MAYOR'S MESSAGE

To all our dear friends who have come to visit our beautiful town of Pau, I wish you all an excellent stay with us. We invite you to discover our historical and cultural heritage, enjoy a stroll on e Boulevard des rénées in order to kindle the first emotions lt by the many English ho came to Pau in the th century. Indeed, they ave left us with their rchitectural influence, eir traditions still noticeable today...

Welcome to the Royal City at the foot of the Pyrénées,

séjour parmi nous, vous invitant à parcourir notre patrimoine historique, culturel et apprécier les promenades sur le Boulevard des Pyrénées et retrouver ainsi les premières émotions des anglais venus nombreux à Pau au XIXème siècle. En effet ceux–ci nous ont laissé leur empreinte architecturale, leurs traditions encore visibles aujourd'hui...

Bienvenue dans la Cité Royale au pied des Pyrénées.

André Labarrère
Senator & Mayor of Pau,
Former Secretary of State.
Sénateur Maire de Pau,
Ancien Ministre.

Pau Pyrénées Region

Text: Robin Gauldie

Text editor: Anna Brosnan

Cartography: With special thanks to Pau Tourist Board

Advertising: Mellor Media Ltd.

Design: Suzanne Murray

Production: Mark Webster

Translation Services: Magali Berbey-Anderson
email: frenchsolutions@eircom.net

Photography: Copyright Office de Tourisme de Pau/DG N. Sabathier, except pages 70, 74 Destination Bearn de Gave, page 74 CDT Bearn-Pays Basque.

Publishing Information:
This second edition was published in 2004
by Premier Guides Ltd., Envision House, Flood St., Galway.
Email: info@premierguides.net
Dublin Office: Email: info@selectmedialtd.com

Publishers: Denis Lane & Robert Heuston

Typeset in Meta and ATRotis Serif 55
ISBN: 1-904895-04-2
Printed in Ireland

If you have any questions, queries or suggestions, we'd be delighted to hear your contributions for the next edition. Please send to updates@premierguides.net

INSIDE THIS EDITION

MAPS

PAU PYRENEES AIRPORT
CCI
PAU BEARN

Welcome to Pau Airport...

Enjoy the new terminal facilities

The inviting shops and restaurants at Pau-Pyrenees airport are the ideal place to relax and spend time before your flight

Restaurants, bar, press

The elegant Airport Restaurants serve food and drinks from 11am to 9pm:

- Fast food and snacks
- The "Cockpit" brasserie serves a variety of hot and cold dishes
- The gourmet's restaurant new menu offers regional cuisine
- The press corner near the bar sells a wide selection of newspapers and magazines (open 7 days a week)

Telephone: +33 (0)5 59 33 33 23 • e-mail: mathilde.dupere@elior.com

Shops

It is the only place in the region where you can buy a variety of wines at producers' prices. The airport shops also sell a wide range of gastronomic and regional products, gifts and souvenirs all year round

Telephone: +33 (0)5 59 33 24 45
e-mail: boutiques-aeroport@wanadoo.fr

Relax and shop before you fly...

AFAQ ISO 9001 VERSION 2000

PAU PYRENEES AIRPORT
64230 Uzein
Tel: **33 (0) 5 59 33 33 00** - Fax: 33 (0) 5 59 33 33 05 - Telex 570948 F
E-mail: contact@pau.aeroport.fr - **www.pau.aeroport.fr**

PAU INTRODUCTION

Small though it is, Pau has plenty of history, an air of tranquil charm and a climate that has attracted visitors since the 1840s. More than that, it is the perfect gateway to Bearn, a region of France that spans the peaks, pistes and mountain streams of the Pyrénées-Atlantiques, picturesque villages, postcard-pretty market towns and villages and age-old places of pilgrimage.

Formerly the capital of the province of Bearn – which is now part of the Department of Pyrénées-Atlantiques – the town stands 130 feet above the valley of the River Pau, which flows out of the high Pyrénées.

The medieval castle is its central landmark and the long Boulevard des Pyrénées, designed in the nineteenth century and lined with tall palm trees, stretches for almost a mile, with a splendid panorama of the mountains.

Perched on a high bluff, the royal Château de Pau is the heart of the old town ('Vieux Pau') and is surrounded by a labyrinth of narrow cobbled streets. Central boulevards radiate from Place Clemenceau, the hub of the town's shopping and business district. The city's modest but lively nightlife is in the Triangle, formed by the rue Castelnau, rue Lespy and rue Emile-Garet.

It was a Scottish doctor, Alexander Taylor, who put Pau on the tourism map when, in 1842, he lauded its unpolluted atmosphere and mellow climate. A wave of British expatriates followed in his footsteps, creating a little England in the heart of France, with their own church, a golf course (the first in France) and a fashionable racecourse, all of which earned the town the nickname 'la ville Anglaise'.

View of the Château over the Gave de Pau

At the height of the 'belle époque' of the late nineteenth century, there were 300 English villas in and around Pau and their owners endowed the city with hundreds of hectares of landscaped parks and private gardens.

That golden age came to an end with the First World War, but the golf course, the racecourse and Pau's immaculate green spaces remain to be enjoyed and the town still has a reputation as a year-round spa centre. In winter, Pau becomes a lively gateway to some of France's best skiing and winter sports areas, with the snow-covered peaks of the Pyrénées gleaming tantalisingly close on the horizon.

It may come as a surprise to learn that peaceful little Pau first stepped onto the historical stage as the royal capital and seat of the Kings of Navarre. The kings held sway over a powerful medieval border kingdom stretching across the Pyrénées that, from the ninth century onwards, was one of the bastions of embattled Christendom against the Moorish conquerors of Spain. Commanding the mountain passes across the Pyrénées and the great pilgrimage route to Santiago de Compostella, tiny Navarre punched well above its weight in the later middle ages.

Its rulers astutely preserved their independence from their more powerful neighbours – Gascony, Castile and Aragon – until the sixteenth century. In 1515, Ferdinand II of Aragon seized the Spanish part of the kingdom and, in 1589, Pau and the French part of Navarre were absorbed into France.

Ironically, the Navarrese tail was soon wagging the French dog. Sixteenth-century France was wracked by religious conflict and the rulers of Navarre became protectors of France's Huguenot reformers.

Born in 1553, Henry of Navarre became the greatest champion of the French Protestant cause and, in 1594 (after a Machiavellian re-conversion to the Catholic faith) he marched into Paris as a bringer of peace. He was crowned Henri IV of France shortly afterwards and became founder of the Bourbon dynasty which ruled France until the Revolution of 1789.

The Bearn region was formally united with France by the Edict of Union signed in Pau by Louis XIII and from the mid-seventeenth century onwards, France and Spain were more or less at peace. The Pyrenean frontier was no longer the setting for skirmishes and sieges, but Pau and its castle retained their royal connection. The Place Royale, midway along the Boulevard des Pyrénées, was commissioned in 1687 by Louis XIV, who was nicknamed the 'Sun King' and was certainly the most successful of all Henri IV's Bourbon inheritors.

Henri IV was not the only local boy to make good. As early as 1370, Gaston Febus, the warrior-hero of Bearn, extended the original medieval castle and Pey de Garros – whose poetry elevated the local dialect into the respected language of literature – became the city's advocate-general in the mid-sixteenth century. He died in Pau in 1585. Jean Bernadotte, one of Napoleon's most successful marshals, was born here in 1763. After his Emperor's fall, he went on to become King of Sweden.

In recent years, Pau has successfully reinvented itself as a lively and youthful university town, with the opening of the University of Pau in 1970. It has also become a hub of France's petrochemical, natural gas and aeronautical engineering industries, mainly thanks to the discovery, in 1951, of a large natural gas reserve at Lacq, not far from Pau.

The University has rejuvenated the city, with a body of 15,000 students, fifty research laboratories and some 4,000 scientists and technicians; it is a city at the cutting edge of European technology. A pioneering citywide broadband network links its high-tech research labs with Pau's many IT and communications companies.

Today, with the advent of cheaper airfares and frequent flights, more people are discovering Pau and making it, and the surrounding region, a year-round holiday destination that offers much more than spas and skiing. The rugged magnificence of the nearby mountains, the pretty valleys of the Pau, Oloron and Adour rivers, farms and vineyards, historic pilgrimage towns – and, of course, a mouth-watering menu of typical regional dishes and a fine local wine list – make this part of the world ideal for touring, trekking and exploring, or just sitting at a sunny café table and watching the world go by.

Currency and Banking

The currency is the Euro (€), which is issued in notes of €500, €100, €50, €10 and €5 and as coins of €1 and €2 and 50, 20, 10, 5, 2 and 1 cent. Sterling is not accepted, but is readily exchanged at banks and at some larger hotels.

Banks are open from 9am to 5pm Monday-Friday but many close for lunch (midday-1.30pm or even 2pm). Most banks have a foreign exchange counter, but it can be quicker to use a bank debit card at an automatic teller machine to withdraw cash directly from your account. Money is dispensed in euros and ATMs accept all credit and debit cards displaying the Maestro/Cirrus symbols. Your bank is likely to make a small charge for this service, but this does not amount to much more than the commission charged in most banks and at bureaux de change.

Recent surveys have revealed that France, far from being one of Europe's most expensive countries, has become one of the continent's cheaper destinations –

Bosquet Centre

on a par with Greece and generally quite a bit cheaper than Britain or Ireland. Not surprisingly, wine, spirits and beer are all much cheaper than in the UK (both in shops and in cafés and restaurants). Hotels, small pensions and chambres d'hotes accommodation are also very reasonably priced compared with their British equivalents.

Be aware that prices do vary a lot. Just as you'd expect at home, some bars, cafés and restaurants are far more expensive than others. On a budget, look out for restaurants with set menus, offering two or three courses with wine at prices that can be a real bargain. In bars and cafés, a coffee or a glass of wine at the bar is cheaper than at a waiter-service table on the terrace. In most places, service is included in the price of your meal or drink ('service compris') but a token tip is always welcome; where you see the sign 'service non compris' (service not included) it's a heavy hint that tipping is expected, but 10% is acceptable.

Transport

With a population of less than 90,000, Pau is not a big city and it can easily be explored on foot. However, to explore the hinterland of the Bearn or head up into the Pyrénées you will probably need a car, as local buses are few and far between on roads off the routes connecting the region's main towns. Roads are generally excellent, with the A64 toll autoroute connecting Pau with Tarbes and with Bayonne, Biarritz and the Atlantic coast.

France's road safety record, on the other hand, is much worse than Britain's. Drive defensively and remember to drive on the right. Note, too, that the permitted blood-alcohol level for drivers is just half of that permitted in Britain (one glass of wine will put you right on the

Café life in Pau

limit) and penalties are severe. Police can demand on-the-spot fines for some traffic offences, including speeding. Speed limits are generally 110 kph on roads designated as RN (routes nationales) and 130 kph (110 in bad weather) on autoroutes. Smaller rural D roads (routes departementales) have lower speed limits and can be steep, narrow and serpentine, though they are well surfaced.

There is a huge public car park on the edge of Pau city centre, and most towns in the region have similar car parks. Using these is always much easier than trying to find somewhere to park in the narrow central streets. Car hire is somewhat cheaper than in the UK and a tank of petrol costs around ten per cent less than in a British filling station.

City buses, operated by **STAP** (Societe des Transports Autocars de Pau, tel: 05 59 14 15 16), connect central Pau with its outer suburbs. They run from 6.30am-10.00pm Monday-Saturday. Multi-trip tickets valid for a day's travel cost €1. You can buy them from the tourist information offices on Place Clemenceau or Place

Royale, or the STAP ticket shop on Rue Gachet. Inter-city buses run from the coach terminal next to the railway station to towns and villages around the Bearn region.

Taxis are metered and congregate outside the railway station. They can be called or booked in advance on 05 59 02 22 22. Taxis are also available for longer trips to nearby towns and villages. A taxi to the airport costs around €20.

Happily, a **funicular railway** connects the station with the Boulevard des Pyrénées high above it. It's free and runs daily from 6.45am-12.10pm, 12.35pm-7.50pm, and

Funicular railway

8.15pm-9.40pm Monday-Friday and 1.30pm-7.50pm and 8.15pm-9.00pm Sundays and bank holidays (closed 25 December, 1 January, 1 May and during the Pau Grand Prix).

SNCF French Railways high-speed trains connect Pau with Bordeaux, Nice, Toulouse, and Lyon. Tel: 0836 35 35 35 or log on to www.sncf.com for information. The railway station is south of the old town centre and about 40 metres below.

Tours

Guided tours of the castle and the historic centre are offered daily in July and August, starting at Place Royale, near the Château, and take approximately one hour and fifteen minutes. For departure times of tours with English-speaking guides, contact the **Pau Municipal Tourism Office**, 2 Rue Henri IV, Place Royale (tel: 05 59 27 27 08, fax: 05 59 27 03 21, email: omt@ville-pau.fr, website: www.ville-pau.fr). Free, guided tours of the historic city council buildings and the municipal gardens can be arranged for groups of ten or more. Tel: 05 59 11 46 64, Mon-Fri.

The Tourism Office can also provide details of escorted coach tours to sights and attractions around the region, including Tarbes and Lourdes and the popular wine route through the vineyards of Jurancon. Out of town, you can take a scenic rail tour to the **Lac d'Artouste** (6,562ft or 2,100m above sea level) on the **Petit Train d'Artouste**.

Also high in the mountains, the **Parc National des Pyrénées** is a pocket of wilderness that shelters the last few bears left in France. Park guides can be contacted on the website www.parc-pyrenees.com Visits to some of the fifty-seven vineyards along the **Jurancon Wine Route** (www.vins-jurancon.fr) can be arranged through the **Commanderie de Jurancon**, tel: 05 59 81 70 30. Guided tours of Oloron Ste-Marie and its historic cathedral can be arranged through the **Oloron Ste-Marie Tourist Office** at www.ot-oloron-ste-marie.fr or call 05 59 39 98 00.

France is well ahead of many European countries, including the UK, in providing access to heritage sites and other attractions for wheelchair users and other people with disabilities. Most of the sights, parks and

Aeroport Pau-Pyrénées

gardens featured in this guide are wheelchair-accessible. For details of access, contact the Tourism Office.

Airport

The modern and efficient **Aeroport International Pau-Pyrénées** handles more than 600,000 passengers per year, with two daily flights from London and nine scheduled return flights daily to Paris. The airport is 7km north of the town centre. **Shuttle buses** operate between the airport, the railway station and the town centre and seats can be booked by telephone on 05 59 02 45 45. Buses leave the airport at 1.30pm Friday-Monday and 2.50pm Tuesday-Thursday and leave the station 11.15am Friday-Monday and half past midnight Tuesday-Thursday. Stops en route are Cours Lyautey (for the university), Place de Verdun and Place Clemenceau. The fare is €5 one-way, €9 return.

Facilities in the terminal include an airport shop which sells regional produce include wines, Armagnac, foie gras, Spanish hams and sausages and other local specialties. The airport also has a restaurant, snack bar, newsagent and tobacconist. All facilities are open seven days a week. Airport information: tel: 05 59 33 33 00, www.pau.aeroport.fr.

PAU CITY CENTRE

The best place to start exploring Pau is the **Place Royale** in the heart of the old quarter. The most effective way to do it is on foot. You'll find the helpful **Municipal Tourist Office** at 2 Rue Henri IV, on the northwest corner of this elegant square. The main attractions in this part of town are the 900-year-old castle, the historic private mansions of the castle quarter and the restored sixteenth-century home of the **Parliament of Navarre**.

The grand Place Royale has a chequered history. It was first laid out in 1767 during the reign of France's 'Sun King', **Louis XIV**, but a church dedicated to France's eponymous patron saint was never begun. The statue of Louis XIV, which stood in the centre of the square, was pulled down during the Revolution and the square wasn't completed in its present style until the mid-nineteenth century.

From the Place Royale, it's a short walk down **Rue Henri IV** (heading west) to the **Château**, Pau's most spectacular historic landmark. Pau still feels a special fondness for Henri IV, who was born here in 1553 and who is called 'nostre Henric' ('our Henry') in local dialect. The castle was founded some 500 years before his birth and his successors went on adding to it and endowing it with new treasures.

You enter the castle by crossing the **Pont de Gramont**, over a deep ravine that added to the stronghold's natural defences. To the left as you cross the bridge is the oldest part of the castle complex; the sturdy keep built by Count Gaston III of Foix, known as **Gaston Febus**, during the fourteenth century.

Between this and the much later **Napoleon III**, built in the nineteenth century, there is a statue of Henri IV by

the eighteenth-century sculptors **Barthelemy Tremblay** and **Germain Gissey**, which stands guard over the entrance to the inner castle complex.

Slate-roofed towers stand above the cobbled main courtyard and inside the royal chambers is one of the world's finest collections of **Gobelins tapestries** – almost one hundred glowing, intricately-woven wall hangings – chosen during the nineteenth century from the royal collections of **King Louis-Philippe** and the Emperor Napoleon III, both of whom added new wings to the castle during their reigns.

Salles des Cents Couverts, Royal Hall of Louis Philippe, in Château de Pau

In the southern wing of the castle are the private chambers built for Napoleon III and for **Queen Jeanne d'Albret** (mother of Henri IV) and the room in which the future founder of the **Bourbon royal dynasty** was born, where you can still see the turtle shell in which he was rocked as a new-born baby. Below the terrace, on the south side of the castle, a steep glacis – built to resist artillery bombardment – overlooks formal **Renaissance gardens** laid out by Queen Jeanne in memory of her husband, **Antoine de Bourbon**. During the sixteenth century, the castle park and gardens were famed all over Europe for their elegance.

Château de Pau The grand chambers of the West Wing were elegantly redecorated by King Louis-Philippe for his Queen, **Marie-Amelie** and were later favoured by Napoleon III's Empress, **Eugenie de Montijo**. They are still known as the **Empress's Chambers**. The **Billere Tower**, the castle's northwest bastion, houses a fine collection of nineteenth-century paintings.

Parliament of Navarre (Conseil-Generale)
When **Louis XIII** formally united Bearn with France in 1620, the former **Law Courts of Navarre** – opposite the Château, at the foot of Rue Henri IV – became the seat of the regional council of nobles; the Parliament of Navarre. Restored to its former glory, with a dramatically designed new annex, the building now serves as the home of the Pyrénées-Atlantiques regional administration. East of the Parliament building are the **Gassion Mansion**, a splendid belle époque building, and the **Church of St Martin**, built in the nineteenth century and dedicated to Pau's patron saint.

The Castle Quarter – east of the Château – was the original heart of **'Vieux Pau'**, but isn't quite as old as it looks. It was extensively rebuilt in the sixteenth to nineteenth centuries. Nevertheless, it is studded with dozens of fine historic buildings. Virtually in the shadow of the castle, the **Maison de Peyre** (or Maison de Sully) is an elegant seventeenth-century mansion, which was the Pau residence of Henry IV's closest advisor, the **Comte de Sully**. Give a pat to the doorknocker in the shape of a curly-tailed hound as you pass – it's said to bring you luck. Almost opposite, at 5 rue du Château, is the birthplace of one of France's most famous soldiers, **Jean de Gassion**.

There's more historic architecture on the **Rue du Moulin**, where tall townhouses display architectural features from periods as early as the eleventh century. **Rue Joffre**, lined with lovely seventeenth- and eighteenth-century mansions, leads to Pau's oldest square, **Place Reine-Marguerite**, which is lined with arched arcades, some of them dating from the late fifteenth century. This was the market square of medieval Pau. It was also where criminals were publicly executed and, during the years of the **'Terror'** that followed the **French Revolution**, this is where the guillotine stood.

Place Reine Marguerite

South of the Château

South of the Château (and far below it) the **Gave de Pau** stream is dotted with small islands and lined with palms and landscaped gardens. These are just some of the parks that give Pau more greenery than most European cities, with a generous 80 square metres of park and garden per head of population.

On the **Place de la Monnaie**, the solid-looking **Tour de la Monnaie** (Mint Tower) was the royal mint of the Bearn region until the Revolution, minting gold, silver and copper coinage with the vaqueta (calf) of Bearn on one side and the king's profile on the other. The **Camp Batailhe**, next to the tower, was a popular medieval

Gassion mansion from the Jardin St Martin

venue for duels between hot-blooded young noblemen. In the sixteenth century, when Pau was a magnet for Huguenot reformers, it was the scene of equally heated quarrels between religious factions.

Below the Tour de la Monnaie, a footpath goes along the **Heid Canal,** built in the fifteenth century to power the royal flourmills. This path leads to the superbly designed modern gardens of the **Pyrénées-Atlantiques departmental authority headquarters.** Entering from the west, you pass through water gardens with palms, ponds and trachycarpus trees – originally from the Himalayas, but grown in Pau since 1857 – profuse plantings of flowering shrubs and potted palms, and two graceful Japanese gardens.

The **Funiculaire de Pau** was built in 1908 so it's comforting to know that this antique cable railway connecting the Place Royale with the canal and gardens south of the centre was renovated in 1978. The **Joantho Gardens,** east of the funicular station, were laid out between 1888 and 1908, and are lushly planted with palm trees, mimosas and banana plants. You might almost be on the Riviera, especially in spring and early summer when the air is filled with the scent of mimosa blossoms.

To the east of the gardens, the **Avenue Napoleon Bonaparte** is planted with exotic cacti, yuccas and agaves from Mexico, all of which flourish in Pau's mellow climate despite the occasional dusting of winter snow. From here, you can stroll back up to the **Boulevard des Pyrénées** by the steeply climbing **Sentiers du Roy.**

Across the canal from the funicular terminus is the railway station, with connections westward to **Bayonne** and **Biarritz,** northwest to **Bordeaux** and east to **Toulouse.** Beyond the south bank of the Gave de Pau lie the city's residential suburbs.

North of the Château

North of the Château de Pau lie the oldest parts of 'Vieux Pau' and its modern commercial hub, main shopping streets and nightlife district, along with some of the town's most important historic and cultural museums.

The **Porte Corisande** (Corisande Gate) is named after one of Henri IV's many mistresses. Its arched gateway and imposing brick gate-towers once marked the northern limits of the walled city. Corisande (Diane Corisande d'Andoins) was the widow of the **Duke of Gramont**. A shrewd politician as well as a patron of French poets and intellectuals, her advice helped Henri on his way to the throne of France. West of the Porte is the gracious Place Gramont, an early urban design project initiated in 1779 by the town planner **Francois Flamichon**. He died before the work was completed and it was finally finished in 1838. Originally named in honour of Henri IV, it was later renamed after the Duc de Gramont, an eighteenth-century descendant of Corisande who supported Flamichon's original grand scheme.

East of the Place, the **Bernadotte Museum** is named after one of Pau's most successful sons. **Jean-Baptiste Bernadotte**, born here in 1763, became a Marshal of France under **Napoleon Bonaparte**. In 1810, five years before Napoleon's final defeat, he was invited by the Swedish Parliament to take the vacant throne of Sweden, which he ruled until his death. One of his descendants is on the Swedish throne today. His birthplace has been preserved (and restored) very much as it was 200 years ago, with a working eighteenth-century kitchen and a collection of weapons, battle-plans, portraits, period furniture and works of art.

It's well worth strolling through the **Hedas quarter**, just south of the Musée Bernadotte, for a look at some of Pau's oldest buildings. This part of town has a rich heritage of medieval architecture and grew up around the spring, which provided the earliest town-dwellers with fresh water. It's nowhere near as lively now as it must have been during the Middle Ages, when it was a conglomeration of taverns, inns, livestock markets, slaughterhouses and tanneries, but nor is it as malodorous as it was then. Look out for the old houses on **Rue Rene Fournets**, some of which have stone staircases, inner courtyards or carved door arches dating back to the fifteenth and sixteenth centuries.

North of the **Chemin du Hedas**, you pass quickly from the Middle Ages into the modern world, entering the modern **Bosquet quarter**. This formerly run-down part of the city centre was the target of an ambitious urban regeneration scheme during the 1990s, when it was transformed into an up-market shopping district. **Les Halles**, the original site of the town's produce market, is now a block of smart food stores specialising in the wines, cheeses, meat and dairy products of the region, while the broad **Place de la Republique** hosts an appealing open-air market where farmers and traders bring their fresh produce. It is at its liveliest – and most colourful and photogenic – on Saturday mornings. To experience it in full swing, you need to get there early as it kicks off at around 7.30am and winds down around midday, when buyers and vendors alike adjourn to the nearby cafés for an extended and well-earned lunch break.

East of the Château

One of the sights you simply must explore while in Pau is the Boulevard des Pyrénées, which stretches eastward from the castle for the better part of 2km.

Until Napoleon's time, the southern wall of the Place Royale shut off one of France's grandest views. Bonaparte, in a typically imperious gesture, had the wall demolished to reveal a stunning panorama of Pyrenean peaks. The Boulevard, with its abundance of palm trees, was laid out towards the end of the nineteenth century by the architect **Jean-Charles Alphand**, who designed many of Paris's best-loved avenues and public spaces. Year-round, the Boulevard des Pyrénées is a riot of colourful blooms, but it is arguably at its most beautiful in May and June when Pau and its surrounds are lush with summer flowers and foliage and the high sierras of the Pyrénées on the horizon still gleam with the last of the winter snow. The finest viewpoint along the Boulevard is **the Belvedere**, where the poem 'Le Cor', by **Alfred de Vigny**, is carved in stone – just one of many verses by Romantic poets who were inspired by the view. The **Table d'Orientation** balustrade that runs along the south side of the Boulevard is labelled with the names of mountains; line up the label with the highest summit beyond it to identify each peak by name.

Midway along the Boulevard des Pyrénées, the **Square George V** is a monument to Franco-British friendship and the long-standing love affair between Pau and Britain that has been given a fresh fillip by the introduction of low-fare flights to the city.

North of the Square is **Place Clemenceau**, the hub of Pau's busiest shopping district. In the centre of the square stands **La Source** (The Spring), a fine piece of Art Deco statuary.

At the eastern end of the Boulevard stands the **Casino** of the **Palais Beaumont**, where dashing English gentlemen gambled away their family fortunes at the turn of the last century. You can still enjoy a flutter here, although the atmosphere is perhaps a little more subdued than it was when the more daring, high-society set came to France to escape the restraints of Edwardian England. The Palais was built in 1900 to cater to the idle rich of Britain and northern Europe, many of whom wintered in luxurious villas in Pau. As well as housing the gaming salons of the Casino, it is now a thoroughly modern conference and exhibition centre.

Parc Beaumont Casino

Within sight of the Palais Beaumont is a very different institution, the **Jesuit College**, founded almost four centuries ago. In 1620, **Louis XIII** re-imposed Catholicism on Pau, which had for more than a century been France's Protestant stronghold. The Jesuit order founded the College as a spearhead of the Catholic faith, but met a lukewarm response. They left in 1763 and their college is now a high school; the Lycee Louis Barthou.

The **Parc Beaumont**, which surrounds the belle-epoque buildings of the Palais Beaumont and the Casino, is a gorgeously grandiose public space that epitomises the nineteenth-century French vision of an 'English' garden. While English gardeners were obsessively mowing and rolling their greens in pursuit of the perfect lawn, French landscape architects were creating delightful artificial wildernesses that were in sharp contrast to the highly formal Renaissance and Italianate gardens of earlier centuries. Pau's city fathers bought the park from **Anna, Comtesse de Noailles**, in 1876 and, in 1898, commissioned **Henri Martinet** to make it over into a 'jardin Anglais'. He laid out a network of paths radiating from a central bandstand and meandering round a lake stocked with swans, mandarin ducks and other ornamental waterfowl. Martinet imported exotic trees from around the world, including monkey-puzzles from South America, tall sequoias from California, flowering Judas trees, chestnuts and magnolias. Many of the original specimens, now grown to record heights, tower over the gardens.

North of the park is Pau's **Musée des Beaux-Arts** (Fine Arts Museum), a typical piece of elaborate 1930s Art Deco municipal architecture, which houses a remarkably diverse collection of works of art spanning six centuries. In pride of place is **Degas's** 'Le Bureau de coton a la Nouvelle-Orleans' (The New Orleans Cotton Office),

Escapades d'authenticité

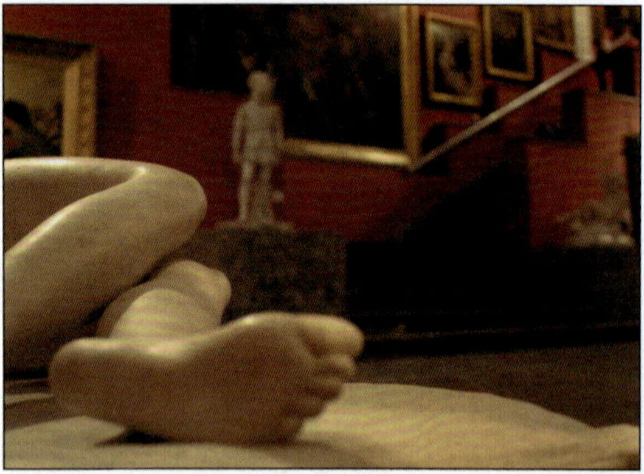

Musée des Beaux-Arts

along with works by **Rubens, El Greco, Giordano, Flandrin** and many more masters from the French, Italian, Flemish, Spanish and Dutch schools. The museum also exhibits the work of Bearnais painters including **Laborde, Poumeyrol** and **Galos**, all of whom worked and lived in Bearn. Three or four visiting art exhibitions are organised every year.

West of the Château

West of the Château lies yet another of Pau's many immaculately maintained areas of greenery; the thickly wooded **Parc du Château**. The **Pont de Nemours** leads from the west side of the castle, across the **Rue Marca** to the gardens known as the **Basse-Plante** or 'low plantations' and the lovely Parc. This huge expanse of aristocratic gardens was first laid out in the sixteenth century, during the reign of **Antoine de Bourbon**, father of Henri IV, who oversaw the planting of more than 2000 trees. Antoine's fondness for horticulture made the park – like the manicured Renaissance gardens south of the Château – famous throughout Europe. His son Henri and daughter Catherine appear to have inherited his passion, bringing in Spanish gardeners to plant pomegranate, lemon, myrtle and orange trees around the castle.

However, Henri's Bourbon successors and their hangers-on lost interest in the park during the eighteenth century when the new court of Louis XIV, the **'Sun King'**, at Versailles drew all aristocratic eyes to Paris. The park and gardens gradually fell into disuse. After the French Revolution, they were rescued for the people of Pau when the estate was sold to a company of Palois who set about restoring the estate as a public pleasure garden.

With the restoration of the Bourbon dynasty after the fall of Napoleon, the park was sold back to the Crown on condition that local people would still be able to use it and the Pont de Nemours was constructed to link the park with the Château gardens. The park stretches for several miles along the north bank of the Gave de Pau and, if you're really keen to stretch your legs, you could follow its walking trails all the way to the Billere golf course on the outskirts of the city, the **Laroin lakes** at **Biron**, or the **Saligues de Pau wetlands** along the margins of the river.

One of the most popular walks through the Parc du Château follows the **'Madame' trail**, named in honour of **Catherine de Navarre**, sister of Henri IV. The walk is lined by more than 200 lime and plane trees, and by beech trees that have been pruned and trained over centuries into strangely contorted shapes. It is a delightful stroll at any time of year.

Beyond the Parc, 5km west of the city, the **Pau Billere Golf Club** is the oldest in mainland Europe. It was built in 1856 by British Army engineers at the request of the town's expatriate community. The 18-hole course is wooded, with 5,314 yards of greens and fairways along the river bank. Visitors are welcome.

PAU SURROUNDS

Pau's modern outskirts contrast sharply with the quaintness of the medieval quarters around the Château and the belle-époque grandeur of the nineteenth-century boulevards.

The university and technical quarter lie to the north and west of the historic centre. The gateway to this modern sector has its own landmark. At the Commune roundabout, next to the university campus stands a striking piece of modern public art, **La Poule au Pot**. It's a tribute to Henri IV, whose popular slogan 'a chicken in every pot' made him a hero to the people of France at a time when most monarchs and nobles showed little concern for the welfare of their subjects. Its name is also a play on words. 'Pot' and 'Pau' sound the same in French, so the sculpture, by **Jean-Louis Magendie**, could be called 'the chicken in the pot' or 'the chicken at Pau'. Since the chicken is apparently laying not an egg but a globe, it symbolises the town's ambition to be a world leader in its chosen fields of study and technology.

Medieval Parliament building, Pau

Université de Pau

The **Université de Pau et le Pays d'Adour**, founded in 1970, has built a worldwide reputation as a centre of scientific and technological excellence and its faculties of Physics, Chemistry, Mathematics, Social Science and Town Planning are renowned. With three post-graduate schools, the university also has eight scientific research teams which make an essential contribution to France's **National Scientific Research Body** (CNRS). An equally important contribution is made by technicians and researchers at the **Jean Feger Scientific and Technical Centre.** This hub of the **Total Fina Elf** petro-chemical group's worldwide exploration and development effort employs some 2,000 people and is housed in a modern complex of gleaming glass-fronted laboratories and offices on the Avenue des Lilas, not far from the university.

On the appropriately named **Avenue Copernic** – named after the great seventeenth-century scientist Copernicus – the **Cite Multimedia** is a pilot zone for an adventurous broadband project that links scores of information technology and communications companies who have helped to put Pau at the forefront of European hi-tech research and development.

The modern quarter is also a magnet for sports and music fans. The innovative **Zenith auditorium** was inaugurated in 1992 by no less a figure than France's godfather of rock, **Johnny Halliday**. The auditorium hosts concerts and shows by the biggest international names in music, while the superb acoustics have been praised by some of the world's top symphony ensembles. Next to it, the **Palais des Sports** celebrates Pau's, and the surrounding Bearn's, devotion to sporting activities. Yet another dazzling piece of modern architecture, this arena, with its space-age appearance, is home to Pau's cup-winning basketball team and also hosts numerous other indoor sports fixtures.

East of the city centre, Pau's **National School of Music and Dance** can be found in a former convent which once housed the sisters of the order of **Marie-Reparatrice**. It's a beautiful late nineteenth-century building and is worth visiting for a quick look at the fine mosaics in its two cloisters.

Racing at the Hippodrome

Out of town to the south – almost directly across the Gave de Pau from the SNCF railway station – is an unmissable attraction for anyone who loves horses. The **Haras de Gelos** is France's premier national stud farm. It was created by Napoleon Bonaparte in 1808 to supply breeding stock to mount the elite cavalry of the Emperor's armies. Today there are around 100 stallions in the paddocks and stables of the farm, ranging from blue-blooded Arabs and thoroughbreds to shaggy, pint-sized Shetlands and sturdy Basque mountain-ponies. The stud farm is based at the former mansion of the president of the Parliament of Navarre, a gracious eighteenth-century building. If you visit in winter, it is possible to take a carriage ride behind a thoroughbred pair, or to ride some of the more docile horses.

A little further out of Pau to the southeast at **Bizanos** – once a separate village, now virtually a suburb of the city – stands the 600-year-old **Château de Franqeville**. Originally, it was the home of the medieval **Lords of Bizanos**, but in 1854 it was acquired by **Albert, Comte de Franqueville**, a Norman aristocrat with a passion for botany and a love of the mountains. As well as making the first ascents of some of the most challenging peaks in the Pyrénées – including **Mt. Netou**, the highest summit in the Pyrenean ranges – he endowed the castle with a beautiful garden of exotic flowers, trees and shrubs. Acquired by the municipality of Bizanos in 1988, the castle and its grounds are a popular venue for wedding receptions and the castle's grand salons have been turned into an elegant modern conference centre.

There's plenty of countryside within walking or cycling distance of Pau. On the south bank of the Gave de Pau, about 16km from the Château, the Laroin lakes – two artificial reservoirs, one of 13 hectares, the other spanning 35 hectares – are surrounded by a large

View of the Pyrénées

wooded garden which is noted for the largest collection of willow trees in Europe, with more than fifty kinds of weeping willow, as well as thirty different kinds of oak tree and a decorative array of flowering shrubs. The arboretum is at its most beautiful in early summer.

At **Saint-Vincent**, the wheelchair-accessible **Barbary Rose Garden** boasts one of the world's finest collections, with more than 800 varieties of rose. Thanks to Pau's temperate climes, there are roses in bud or in bloom almost all year round, and there is a programme of guided walks for serious rose lovers, rose-growing novices and for visitors who merely want to enjoy the scents and colours of a spectacular rose garden in bloom.

If you have a taste for slightly wilder walks, seek out the **Saligues**, a region of wetlands along the

meandering course of the Gave de Pau. Rich in wild flowers and riverside plants, the Saligues are also a fertile refuge for many native and migrant birds.

For birdwatchers, the **Saligue aux Oiseaux Bird Sanctuary** at Biron offers the opportunity to see white egrets, herons, lapwings, plovers, cormorants and many types of duck and other waterfowl, as well as smaller migrant species of warbler, flycatcher and bunting. The **Lac d'Uzein**, 6km northwest of the town centre and not far from the airport, is another body of water that attracts rafts of water birds and is also popular with local anglers.

Like almost every region of France, the Bearn has its own fine wines and the vineyards of Jurancon, almost within sight of the castle walls, have been producing some of France's finest vintages for more than six centuries. You can sample some of the region's many

Vineyards in autumn

wines at the **Commanderie de Jurancon**, in the **Cave des Producteurs de Jurancon** or at the **Confrerie du Jurancon**, all of which offer educational visits and free tastings of wine from hundreds of local winemakers. By car, you can also follow the **Jurancon Wine Route** ('La Route des Vins de Jurancon'), which visits fifty-seven regional vineyards.

The **Château de Momas**, about 16km northwest of Pau, was a stronghold of the **Viscounts of Bearn** and parts of it, including the original moat, are more than 1,000 years old. More modern, and more appealing to non-historians, are the conservatory gardens with their collection of rare and little known medicinal plants, herbal remedies and forgotten vegetables.

All around Pau, an assortment of historic places of worship testify to the region's rich Christian heritage, with churches and chapels dating back to the eleventh century AD. Even if your tastes do not normally run to

Espace Loisirs les Ô kiri

Au Pays de Pyrène

Les Ô Kiri Avenue du Lac
64800 Baudreix
Tel: 05 59 92 97 73
Fax: 05 59 13 93 77
les-okiri@wanadoo.fr

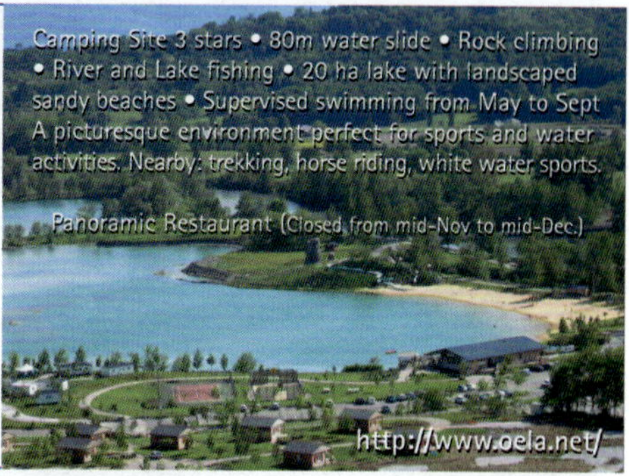

"Unique in the world, Le Musée du Béret is expecting you, situated between Lourdes and Pau, in the heart of the Béarn region, it will no doubt charm you with its authenticity.
Let yourself be tempted! Come and visit us! And if the Béret hat has won your heart, visit our souvenir shop. Why wouldn't you, even if you do not have a baguette, leave our museum wearing a béret?"

Musée du Béret, Place st Roch, 64800 Nay
Tel/Fax: 0559 619170
www.museeduberet.com
E-mail: museeduberet@wanadoo.fr

Le MODERNE

Bar/Restaurant
Icecream Parlour

Nay Town Centre
(half way between Pau and the Pyrenees)
Sun Terrace

Open 7 days - 7.30am-Midnight
Moderne's - Tel. 0033 (0)559 610095

ecclesiastical architecture, the **Cathedrale de Notre Dame** at **Lescar** is worth a visit. Traditionally, the kings of Navarre were buried in the crypt of this elegant little cathedral, which was completed in 1120. Surrounding it are the narrow streets and old stone buildings of one of the region's most evocative historic villages, all encased within a ring of impressive medieval ramparts.

At **Morlaas**, about 5km northeast of Pau, there is the fine eleventh-century church of **Sainte-Foy** (the Holy Faith), which was donated by the Viscounts of Bearn to the monks of Cluny in 1079. Its nave and aisles have survived in their original form. The western gate, with its remarkable stonework, was reconstructed in the nineteenth century after being damaged by fire.

There are other historic churches to be found not much more than a stone's throw from Pau. At **Sevignacq-Theze**, a twelfth-century chapel with a remarkable ornate gateway stands in the shadow of an eighteenth-century Château. At **Larreule**, you'll find a ruined transept and chancel that mark the site of a tenth-century **Benedictine Abbey**. And, at **Sauvelade**, the chapel and bell-tower of the **Church of the Assumption** date from the twelfth century.

GREATER BEARN REGION

Château by night

South of Pau, the foothills and valleys of the Pyrénées beckon and the fertile farmland of the Bearn is studded with picturesque historic towns, villages, castles and, of course, vineyards. Throughout the region, there are lively open-air markets where you can sample and buy local produce. Some of the most colourful are to be found at Arudy, Nay, Orthez, Navarrenx, Salies de Bearn and Oloron Sainte-Marie.

Among other claims to fame, the region was the homeland of **Alexandre Dumas's 'Three Musketeers'**, or at least to the real-life swashbucklers on whom he based the characters of **Porthos** (born in Pau), **Athos** (born near Sauveterre), and **Aramis** (in real life, Henri d'Aramitz, Abbot of Baretous).

Keen walkers can follow the age-old, way-marked pilgrimage paths that lead through the fields and pastures of Bearn to **Santiago de Compostella** in northern Spain. The **Voie du Puy**, which passes through Arthez-de-Bearn, Sauvelade and Navarrenx on its way south, crosses the Pyrénées by the spectacular mountain pass at Roncevaux. The **Voix d'Arles**, leads from Morlaax and Lescar just north of Pau and passes through Oloron Sainte-Marie and south through the mountains to Spain.

The beautifully preserved medieval town of **Oloron Sainte-Marie**, 30km south of Pau, is best known for its twelfth-century cathedral, which has been designated as a **UNESCO World Heritage Site**. The **Cathedrale de Sainte Marie** is a superb example of Gothic ecclesiastical architecture, with magnificent twelfth-century sculpture and a nave. The choir here dates back to the fourteenth and fifteenth centuries. A newly-opened exhibition of church treasures is eye-catching and the cathedral is surrounded by well-kept gardens.

Equally steeped in history is the **Eglise Sainte Croix** (Holy Cross), built at the end of the eleventh century. From this hilltop church there is a fine view over the tiled roofs and narrow streets of the old walled quarter of Oloron to the Pyrénées.

Nearby, the sturdy **Tour de Grede** is one of the surviving bastions of the walled town and also has a panoramic view of Oloron. Next to it, the **Maison du Patrimoine d'Oloron et du Haut Bearn** is a museum which highlights the region's history from prehistoric times to the present day, with a collection of portraits, archaeological and mineralogical displays, and a permanent exhibition featuring the infamous **World War II internment camp at Gurs**.

Also worth a visit is the **Voyage au centre de la Terre** (Journey to the Centre of the Earth) exhibition next to the tourist office at Allees du Comte de Treville. It is an exhibition of glittering minerals, crystals and semi-precious stones from the caves and grottos of the Pyrénées, collected by local geologist **Jean-Paul Save**.

Heading on south towards the Pyrénées, the village of **Arudy** on the banks of the **Gave d'Ossau** is a great place to find out more about the folklore and traditions of the Bearn.

The **Maison d'Ossau Museum** at Arudy is housed in a former abbey and is packed with fascinating displays. It also features an exhibition and film about the **Parc National des Pyrénées**, the nearby pocket of wilderness which straddles the Franco-Spanish border and is home to southern Europe's last few brown bears, huge lammergeyer vultures and dozens of rare bird, flower and butterfly species.

At **Beaucens** near Lourdes, free-flying eagles and falcons soar amid Pyrenean grandeur at the exciting **Donjon des Aigles**, the region's finest bird park. For a soaring panorama, visit the region's highest summit, the **Pic du Midi** and its unique mountain-stop museum space, which opened in 2001 and attracts more than 100,000 visitors a year.

A giddy switchback road leads from the main D934 south of Arudy to the tiny hamlet of **Gere-Belesten**, perched on a steep hillside. This is the home of the **Fromagerie Pardou**, where more than seventy cheese-makers of the Ossau Valley send their wares to be matured in the carefully monitored coolness of a former railway tunnel. With room for more than 20,000 cheeses in high season, the smell is mouth-watering and you can sample as many as you like before you buy.

Between Pau and Lourdes, fortified medieval bastide villages are dotted across the rolling fields of the **Plaine de Nay**. Stop off at Nay for a coffee or a glass of wine and a stroll around the 700-year-old ramparts built to keep out English marauders.

Don't miss the more modern attractions, like the **Musée du Beret**, where you can see French hats being made just as they have been for almost 200 years. To the Bearnais, the beret is much more than just a head-covering; it's an impromptu shopping basket for collecting eggs or wild mushrooms, a handy oven glove and it's so waterproof it can even be used as a bucket to give a thirsty horse a drink!

Park and gardens

For a look at bygone Bearn, visit the **Maison Carree**, an elegant Renaissance mansion in the centre of the village that now houses a folk museum full of antique furniture, farm equipment and old-fashioned tools and household goods.

There's more history at the dinky fourteenth-century **Château de Coarraze**, where **Henri of Navarre** spent his childhood and at the wonderfully eclectic **Musée du Patrimoine des Peres de Betharram,** in Lestelle-Betharram. Here, a glorious clutter of fossils and semi-precious stones, old coins and notes, prehistoric stone tools, embroidery and other handicrafts are crammed into the rooms of a seventeenth-century monastery.

If you are travelling with children, two manmade attractions near **Lestelle-Betharram** are guaranteed to please the whole family. You may not be expecting to see kangaroos, gibbons, or snow leopards in southern France, but the **Zoo d'Asson** has all of these and more in a huge park which was created more than thirty-five years ago. It now houses more than 500 rare and endangered birds and animals, including the kangaroos and lemurs that roam free in the grounds.

Kids will also enjoy the train and boat trip through the **Grottes de Betharram,** an awesome complex of natural caverns full of weirdly-shaped rock formations.

Further into the mountains, the **Train Touristique du Lac d'Artouste** is another fabulous family outing, with open miniature carriages to take you on a 10km scenic ride to an altitude of 1,991m – making it the highest narrow-gauge railway in Europe. The trip includes a cable-car ride and a stop at the pretty (but chilly) **Artouste Lake.** At **Laruns,** the twelfth-century **Château de Beost** was the sixteenth-century home of **Henri d'Aramitz,** the real-life cavalier on whom Dumas based one of his 'Three Musketeers'. The tumbledown castle is being restored by local volunteers, but it's worth visiting just for its splendid location among the peaks.

For many visitors to the region, however, the main attraction is the world's most-visited place of Christian pilgrimage. The faithful have flocked to the grottos and sanctuaries of **Lourdes** ever since 1858, when the **Virgin Mary** appeared to a fourteen-year-old shepherd girl named **Bernadette Soubirous** in a cave close to the banks of the fast-flowing Gave de Pau. Over the next four years, the Virgin appeared repeatedly to Bernadette and the miraculous grotto is now the site of a complex of chapels and sacred shrines, including the **Basilique du Rosaire**, built in 1899, and the cavernous **Basilique de Saint-Pie X**, built in 1958, which can hold a congregation of 30,000.

Saint Bernadette's humble birthplace

Basilique du Rosaire

As well as these sacred sites, Lourdes has a cluster of small religious museums, including: a waxwork museum dedicated to the lives of Bernadette and other saints, Bernadette's humble family home on the Rue des Petits-Fosses, and a model of Lourdes as it was in the mid-nineteenth century, before it was taken over by mass religious tourism.

Religion aside, a visit to the Lourdes region is inspiring, surrounded as it is by rugged mountains where flocks of sheep graze on lush summer pastures criss-crossed by fast-flowing mountain streams.

Greater Bearn Region North (Bearn-Adour)

The **Adour river** runs through Bearn's rugged north, known in the old local dialect as the **Vic-Bilh Montaneres,** or the 'old mountain country'. This region of woods, fields and vineyards is home to both Madiran and Pancherenc grapes, which are unique to the Bearn, and there are plenty of gastronomic treats in the farming villages and market towns.

Fine old sixteenth-century manors stand amid the farmland and old Bearnais traditions, crafts and activities are still strong here. You'll see villagers playing ninepins on the village square instead of the boules (or petanque) that is played everywhere else in France. You should also spot many prosperous-looking old farmhouses with whitewashed walls and red-tiled roofs.

The Compostella pilgrims trudged their way across this region too, and many of the local churches bear the scallop-shell symbol of the pilgrimage route. At **Arzacq**, the ancient walls of **Larreule Abbey** sheltered weary pilgrims.

The region's most striking monument is the delightfully elegant and beautifully preserved **Château de Mascaraas,** near the old fortified town of **Garlin**. Mascaraas was built during the sixteenth and seventeenth centuries and its grand salons retain their authentic eighteenth-century décor, original furniture and works of art. If you visit only one château during your trip through the Bearn, this should be it. The main living room is adorned with painted scenes from mythology and His Lordship's bedroom still has its original Gothic sculptures. Across the Adour river, in the pretty village of **Caupenne d'Armagnac**, the medieval **Château d'Izaute** is also well worth a detour into the Gers region and the heart of Armagnac country.

As it was built in a time when strong walls were more important than gracious living, the **Château de Montaner** is perhaps less elegant. This château was the fourteenth-century keep of the free-booting **Gaston Phebus** (1331-1391), who took the opportunity of the long wars between England and France to maintain his own princedom of Bearn against both rival kingdoms. The fifteenth- and sixteenth-century wall-paintings in Gaston's chapel of St Michael, next to the castle, are superb works of religious art in faded, but still impressive, colours.

Just as exciting is a visit to the **Château de Morlanne,** where art historians Raymond and Helene Riter have lovingly and painstakingly restored a fourteenth-century castle and furnished it with antique furniture and fine paintings by **Fragonard, Canaletto** and other masters.

The region also has plenty of mementos of everyday life in bygone times. Its strongly-flowing rivers were ideal for water-milling and you can visit working mills that have been in use for up to five centuries at **Moulin de Garos**, in the village of **Garos**, and at **Moulin de Bellegarde**, in **Lespielle**.

Greater Bearn Region Northwest

Exploring the region northwest of Pau is easy. The main E80 autoroute between Pau and the Atlantic coast leads straight to **Orthez,** which is the gateway to this region of farmland, fortified medieval towns that would look appropriate on the cover of a sword-and-sorcery epic and wooded river valleys watered by streams that are rich in trout and salmon. Orthez, former capital of the Bearn, is an enchanting little riverside town that for centuries has been a resting-place for weary pilgrims on the long and winding road to Santiago de Compostella. Today, it is peaceful and postcard-pretty at any time of year. Climb to the terrace of the 33-metre-tall tower of the **Château Moncade** for super views of the old town and the jagged Pyrénées off to the south, which must have been a daunting sight for medieval pilgrims who had to hike across the high mountain passes on their way to Spain. Also worth a visit are the **Maison Chrestia,** an elegant eighteenth-century building that is now a museum dedicated to the poet **Francs Jammes,** who lived here between 1897 and 1907, and the **Musée Jeanne d'Albert,** which traces the history of the **Huguenots,** the **Wars of Religion** and the **Reformation** in France.

Not far from Orthez – just off the E80 autoroute at Biron – is another delight for wildlife enthusiasts. Rare migrant wildfowl and wading birds are drawn to the natural beauty of the **Saligue aux Oiseaux,** a 24-hectare expanse of carefully managed wetlands which is a carpet of colourful wild flowers in spring and summer.

With its mineral-rich waters, **Salies de Bearn** is a spa town with hotels and clinics that offer a range of state-of-the-art therapies and natural health and beauty treatments. You can taste local products made with the rock-salt for which Salies is famous, visit the **Musée du Sel,** which traces the history of the salt industry that made the town wealthy and wonder at the collection of strange implements from vanished trades in the interesting **Musée des Arts et Traditions Bearnaises.**

Lush greenery surrounds **Sauveterre de Bearn,** a fortified town with a rich medieval heritage beside the fast-flowing Gave d'Oloron, which is crossed by a fortified stone bridge. Visit the island of **la Glere** with its outstanding gardens, the ruined castle built by the viscounts of Bearn almost 900 years ago, the sturdy **Monreal tower,** with its views of the Gave, and the dramatic fortified arsenal and **Fortress of Tolose.** Times of old come to life within the **Chapelle de Sunarthe,** where a perfect scale model of the twelfth-century city gives you a bird's eye view of a medieval community in miniature.

Nearby, it's worth making a detour to the **Château de Laas,** which has a magnificent collection of richly coloured tapestries and paintings by **Breughel, Rubens** and **Fragonard,** all housed in a jewel of a seventeenth-century manor, surrounded by immaculate landscaped gardens on the banks of the Gave d'Oloron.

Like Sauveterre, picturesque **Navarrenx** owes its ring of ramparts to the turbulent years of the **Hundred Years War** between France and England. Its solid ramparts look impregnable and have served as a backdrop for more than one medieval romance made by the French film and TV industry. For a glimpse into the past, visit the **Navarrenx a Travers les Siecles** display, which tells the tale of the earliest fortifications and the pilgrims' trail to Compostella. Children will like the scale model of the old fortress-town.

Nearby, the **Château de Mongaston,** built in the thirteenth century, looks well preserved for its age,

mainly due to the fact that it was completely restored in 1999. It is surrounded by manicured lawns and a fascinating garden of herbs and medicinal plants, laid out in the style of a twelfth- and thirteenth-century monastery garden. Its lavishly appointed rooms are embellished with vintage furnishings and works of art, along with a series of tableaux of characters from history, each dressed in hand-made costumes appropriate to their era. An excellent spot to take the family on a rainy day, the château also has its own tea-room.

Just a few kilometres south of Navarrenx, the World War II internment camp at **Gurs** stands as a grim memorial to a tragic era in French history. The camp was the biggest in southern France and more than 60,000 men, women and children were imprisoned here between 1939, when Spanish and Basque republicans fleeing fascism in Spain became the first internees, and 1944-5, when France was liberated. Ironically, the last prisoners behind Gurs' barbed wire were German soldiers captured by the Allies in the final weeks of the war.

PROPERTY

Easy access to Pau by air from the UK has generated a huge wave of interest in property around the region from British visitors in search of a place in the sun. For many, the option of buying a second home or even moving lock, stock and barrel to the Bearn is certainly tempting and, despite the slowing of the UK property market, bricks and mortar in Pau and the Pyrénées still look like a fantastic bargain to many buyers when compared with the price of homes in the UK.

Perhaps even more important than house prices is the quality of life. So many of the good things cost so much less in France than they do in the UK and the French pace of life makes it possible to savour them.

Property has substantially increased in value in the region in recent years and, although prices are unlikely rise dramatically in the near future, French property still looks like an attractive investment when compared with its British counterpart, especially with the current uncertainty in the British property market.

For the many would-be expatriates who dream of running their own guesthouses, gîtes or even luxury hotels, the Pyrénées region has one significant advantage over most other parts of France; it has tourism potential virtually year-round. The lucrative winter sports season begins to get underway just as the last leaves of autumn fall but Pau's mellow climate still allows palm trees flourish when the snow lies thick on the Pyrénées.

Whether you are buying as a long-term property investment, planning on retiring to France, looking to launch your own business or just hunting for the perfect holiday hideaway, the rules are much the same as they are at home: location, location and location are the key factors.

Spectacular views or not, a farmhouse in a high mountain valley miles from the shops and other public amenities will command far lower prices than a similar property near a village with all the facilities. More surprisingly, some of the biggest properties on the market are also among the cheapest, at least in terms of Euros per square metre.

There is a vast range of properties on offer from local real estate agents or **'agences immobilieres'** and, although prices have shot up in recent years, there are still plenty of homes on the market at prices that look excitingly affordable when compared with property in most parts of Britain.

Fortunately, a growing number of leading property agencies based in Pau and around the region – such as **Pierre Conchez** and **Euro Pyrénées, Agence Iluro Anglaise, Agence Immobiliere Nicole Malterre, Immo 64, Office Central Immobilier, Abafim, Spring Cottage** and **VINI** – are already well versed in the demands of British customers. Many have English-speaking consultants who can help you find the house, apartment or plot of land that is just right for you, whether in Pau itself, in

one of the beautiful towns and villages nearby, out in the countryside or high in the wilds of the Pyrénées. **Sauveterre de Bearn Immobilier,** for example, based in the pretty medieval town of Sauveterre, has a range of properties between the mountains and the sea. For anyone looking to purchase a property at a bargain price and for those who dream of restoring an old and dilapidated house full of character, companies such as **SERA** offer a fully skilled property renovation service.

You may well be buying a property for cash – always the quickest way – or re-mortgaging property at home to fund your purchase, but it is also worth considering taking out a mortgage from a French supplier. Mortgage interest rates in France have been historically significantly lower than in the UK. In early 2004, mortgages were available for as little as 3.5% and, although interest rates are tipped to rise, they could still be as much as two percentage points below British levels.

The French legal system makes purchasing property surprisingly easy. Basic conveyancing is handled by a lawyer called a 'notaire' whose job is to act as an evenhanded intermediary between buyer, seller and the French state, ensuring that the property comes with clear title and that all relevant taxes are paid. You don't have to hire your own lawyer as the notaire will do the legal minimum, but it is always a good idea to employ a lawyer at home who is familiar with French property law in case of unforeseen legal obstacles or problems with title.

You will be asked for a ten per cent deposit to seal the deal (held by the notaire until completion), at which point the sale becomes legally binding for both buyer and seller, assuming no legal problems arise. Completion should take no more than three months (and often as little as six weeks), after which you'll be ready to take on the challenges of living in France.

Naturally, property is cheapest at the smaller end of the market. Demand is lower for typical village houses,

which are often in need of complete renovation and don't have a garden or adjoining land. A popular option for buyers of such properties is to open up part of the 'grenier' or loft to create a small, sunny roof terrace and, with luck, you'll find somewhere with those stunning Pyrenean views.

House prices vary across an extremely wide range, with Nay-based **Nicole Malterre**, for example, offering some small houses suitable for renovation in secluded mountain valley locations for as little as €20,000. Of course, buyers will need to budget for a lot of essential work.

For those looking for somewhere in a quiet, pretty village, a three-bedroom house needing some renovation could cost as little as €100,000 and **Iluro**, which specialises in finding properties for English-speaking buyers, lists one-bedroom apartments from as little as €78,000 in villages such as picturesque Oloron Ste-Marie, with the price of two-bedroom apartments starting from around €115,000.

Elsewhere, as little as €65,000 might buy an old stone bergerie (shepherd's bothy), high in the hills with a four-hectare spread of sheep pasture – again, however, such properties will require serious investment to make them habitable.

For investors looking to make a serious move to France, investment opportunities in the accommodation sector abound. Indeed, for those willing to invest time, expertise and capital, large properties suitable for use as gîtes, guesthouses or hotels can be surprisingly affordable. As this guide goes to press in late 2004, Iluro has on its books a 10-bedroom former hotel with attached two-bedroom apartment in the Vallee de Baretous for just €244,000.

Buyers in search of a more solid investment – involving less risk and a higher degree of personal comfort – may be drawn to the wide portfolio of more modern properties that also appeal to French buyers, who are generally much more reluctant than the British to invest in old properties for renovation and are more interested in

comfortable, modern second homes which include facilities such as two-car garages, pools and fully-fitted kitchens and utility rooms. At this end of the property ladder, between €400,000 and €500,000 could buy a three-bedroom villa with dining room, lounge, garage, pool and between 1000-2000 square metres of garden. Higher up the scale again, Iluro has properties such as a five-bedroom mansion on the outskirts of Pau with gardens, a pool, 3.5 hectares of grounds – and an asking price of €915,000.

There's a growing level of international sophistication in the French property market, with property agencies like **Abafim** adapting to meet the needs of potential British buyers whose grasp of local rules and customs may be a little shaky. Like most French businesses, many agences immobilieres shut up shop at 17.30 on weekdays, at noon on Saturday and do not reopen until Monday morning. This can be frustrating for British would-be buyers who are accustomed to estate agents staying open all weekend. Abafim, however, prides itself on having English and French staff on hand seven days a week to talk property novices through the legal procedures involved in buying property in France and providing assistance with services such as gas, electricity and

More service
Less fees
Libre immo
Visit freely, from your house and with your family, all the properties of your choice on offer on our web site
PAU
+ 00 33 559 83 91 56
pau@libre-immo.com
OLORON
+ 00 33 559 39 12 46
oloron@libre-immo.com
TARBES
+ 00 33 562 93 73 99
tarbes@libre-immo.com
www.libre-immo.com

telephone and sourcing tradesmen such as plumbers, electricians, and builders. They are also happy to provide assistance with opening bank accounts, obtaining a loan to purchase a property, or even finding somewhere for potential buyers to stay while they look for their dream home.

In many towns and villages there are 'maisons de maitre'. These are the former homes of prosperous local farmers or merchants, sometimes dating from the seventeenth or eighteenth centuries. With two or three large public rooms and up to a dozen bedrooms, they are simply too big to attract many buyers. Converting them into apartments presents some planning issues, and renovation can cost more than the original purchase price. That said, buyers hoping to live the dream of running a guesthouse in France may find 'maisons de maitre' an attractive investment.

Medium-sized, more modern property is often the most expensive, especially if little or no renovation is required and luxuries, such as a pool, have already been installed.

In general, French buyers – whether local people or holidaymakers from northern France – do not share the British obsession with finding a dilapidated property to fix up. They much prefer newly built holiday villas with all mod cons, so if such property is to your taste you may find yourself competing with French buyers and paying a premium price. The same goes for plots of land suitable for the construction of a new property. Naturally, houses with a garden or plot of land also command higher prices.

A compromise solution is to look out for a village house which comes with one or more plots of land on the outskirts of the village (but make sure you have clear legal

SALES • LETTING
MANAGEMENT

Agence
Immo 64

www.immo64.fr

36 Avenue Jean Mermoz,
64000 Pau.
Tel: 0559 727272

Agence de Ean
2 Place de la Marie
Tel: 0559 818080

NAY valley (Site 2900 m²) **REF : 1831** at 301 000€
Very attractive renovated 19thc period house, 4 bedrooms, fully equiped and laid out kitchen, office, fireplace, 17th c outbuildings, Garden. Near all facilities. RARE OPPORTUNITY!

LARGE SELECTION OF MODERN AND CLASSIC HOMES

Sector LEMBEYE (Site 4700 m²)
REF : 1858 at 257,720€
Charm of the countryside. Renovated Bearn farm, 3 bedrooms, office, chalet, outbuildings. Fenced off - MUST BE SEEN!!

Near NAY (Site 1700 m²)
REF : 1697 at 290 200€
Very pretty Bearn house, 4 bedrooms, office, living room with fireplace. Quiet area, Near all facilities.

Sector LASSEUBE (Site 7 hectares)
REF : 1514 at 300 000€
Bearn farm, 6 bedrooms, large living room with fireplace, Barn, Stables.

WEST OF PAU (4500 m²) **REF : 1517** at 528 150€
Magnificent house with large rooms, 4 bedrooms, fully equiped kitchen, living room cum dining area/fireplce, Double garage, Swimming pool, Landscaped garden. good views and bright.

Farmhouse Courtyard

title to these as well as the house). Many village homes have such plots, usually used as vegetable gardens. Not quite as private as your own walled château garden, perhaps, but pleasant enough for summer afternoons in a deckchair or pottering around in your herb garden.

Look out, too, for houses with a 'remise' – a separate lock-up building, usually attached to the main house, originally used for storing tools and farm equipment. In smaller village houses, storage space is usually limited, so an adjoining remise can offer valuable storage space and can sometimes be converted into a utility room to house fridge, freezer and washing machine, or even into a kitchen extension.

The typical Bearnaise country home is a solid, stone-built two-storey affair with six to eight rooms and a red-tiled roof with four slopes. They are undeniably attractive, but beware of rotten woodwork and worm-eaten roof beams. Some giveaway phrases to look out for in the property ads include: 'a refraichir', indicating a house that needs little more than a lick of paint and some plaster and tile work to be habitable; 'travaux a prevoir' which means you must expect some serious building work; and 'grands travaux a prevoir' which means you may be buying little more than four crumbling walls and a leaking roof. Finding local builders and tradesmen to help make your dream into reality can sometimes be time-consuming and frustrating.

The frenzy of property buying and renovation in the region means most masons, electricians, roofers and plumbers have more work than they can handle at short notice. Once you have found a tradesman, he must inspect the work to be done and give you a written 'devis' or price quote for the job. You will be expected to pay a substantial percentage – usually around one-third – up front. The advantage of the French system, however, is that the cost of the job will not suddenly increase once work has begun. Make sure you keep copies of all receipts for renovation, decoration and building work, as you can offset such costs against French capital gains tax if you decide to sell.

Most foreign buyers are looking for village houses or country homes. Both have their own special attractions. A country house may have substantial land and offer glorious isolation, but living at a distance from shops, public transport and other village facilities means you will need to be highly organised about your weekly shopping and you may need to invest in a car or rent a vehicle for the duration of your holiday. Village houses, on the other hand, are more easily accessible and popping out to the shops for a fresh baguette, or to the café for a glass of wine, is painless. However, the downside is a lot less privacy. Your neighbours are likely to be friendly and generous with invitations for an evening 'apero' or a morning coffee.

Bear in mind that some French property experts advise against buying as an investment and that far too many foreign purchasers have fallen into the trap of blithely assuming they can make a living by running their French home as a guesthouse or turning out-buildings into holiday gîtes. Running a guesthouse or gîte rental business is hard work for low profits and is unlikely to produce any income at all for at least eight months of the year.

Furthermore, if you do decide to sell your property, you may well have to pay capital gains tax, which will wipe out any real profit from the appreciation in value of your property – unless, that is, you have established your property as your place of primary residence for French tax purposes. This in turn, however, exposes you to the risk of paying income tax at French levels.

SAUVETERRE DE BEARN

ESTATE AGENCY

Rue Léon Bérard - 64390 SAUVETERRE DE BEARN
Tel : 05 59 38 94 99 Mobile : 06 81 43 70 37
Fax : 05 59 38 87 96
Email : sauveterrebearnimmo@wanadoo.fr

In Sauveterre de Bearn, charming and oustanding properties.

In the pretty medieval village of Sauveterre de Bearn, Claudine LABORDE-SALLENAVE has opened her estate agency (beside the church) since January 2004.

Benefitting from her previous experience working at a solicitor's, she is the right person to advise you when selling or purchasing property.

Orthez architecture

Unless you are lucky enough to be planning your retirement, you will need to look at other ways of making a living in France. One option is working from home via e-mail and the web. France is admirably switched-on when it comes to providing broadband and other IT services locally and France Telecom, the state-owned supplier, is soon to be privatised, so telecommunications services could well become more competitive in the near future.

You may also want to invest in a TV satellite dish, as even fluent French speakers admit that French TV is less than inspiring when it comes to entertainment, news and current affairs. Fortunately, you can have a dish and digi-box fitted for as little as €200.

France is surprisingly user-friendly, even to new arrivals who speak little French. Getting utilities such as electricity, water and phone connected is handled with remarkable promptness, as is opening a bank account. France Telecom even has an area of its website dedicated to English speakers with homes in France. If you do encounter any problems, however, it is likely that your new neighbours will be more than happy to help in any way they can.

PROPERTY

LIBRE – IMMO
36, rue Maréchal JOFFRE
64000 PAU
Tel: 05 59 83 91 56
Fax: 05 59 83 90 44
Email: pau@libre-immo.com
Website: www.libre-immo.com

We welcome you to our estate agency near the Château de PAU. Here you can access all the properties on offer in our BEARN agencies (Pau and Oloron) and BIGORRE agency (Tarbes). Feel free to check out our website for any properties that might be of interest to you.

PIERRE CONCHEZ IMMOBILIER
4 Rue Louis Barthou 64000 PAU
Tel: 05 59 11 11 00
Fax: 05 59 11 11 01
Email: pierreconchezimmo@orpi.com
Website: maison-sud-ouest.com

Pierre Conchez Estate Agency is a member of the number one network of estate agents in France. The agency has permanently at its disposal more than 700 properties to offer, as well as providing a specifically adapted service for our English speaking, German and Spanish customers.

SAUVETERRE DE BEARN ESTATE AGENCY
Rue Léon Bérard - 64390
SAUVETERRE DE BEARN
Tel: 05 59 38 94 99
Mobile: 06 81 43 70 37
Fax: 05 59 38 87 96
Email: sauveterrebearnimmo@wanadoo.fr

We have charming and oustanding properties. Located in the pretty medieval village of Sauveterre de Bearn (beside the church) since January 2004. With years of legal experience we are the right choice to advise you when selling or purchasing property.

SERA
Simon Entreprise
Rénovation Ancien
64 000 Pau
Tel: 06 80 881 635
Email: simon.entpsera@wanadoo.fr

Jean Paul Simon is a craftman. Enjoying 15 years of unequalled experience in all types of renovation works of old houses. All types of work.
Show us your plans and we'll take the project from there.
Translator available.

SKI RESORTS

Pau is the gateway to a winter wonderland of downhill pistes – suitable for skiers at all skill levels, from expert to novice – along with superb long-distance, cross-country trails through Pyrenean valleys and forests and a host of other winter sports and activities. Take the breathtaking, 15-minute cable car ride to the summit of the **Pic du Midi**, the region's highest peak, for an awe-inspiring panorama of some 300 kilometres of snow-covered summits and slopes that will set any winter sports fan's pulse racing.

None of the ski resorts of the Pyrénées are more than 90 minutes drive from Pau-Pyrénées airport, and each of them boasts a full array of excellent places to stay, fine restaurants, and enough après-ski activities to satisfy the most demanding winter sports enthusiast.

Unlike so many top ski areas, Pau and the Pyrénées are also perfect for mixed groups of skiers and non-skiers. Most resorts are strongly family-oriented, with crèches for children too young to enjoy the slopes. For non-skiing grown-ups there are ski bases that offer more than white powder. **Sainte-Marie d'Oloron** is the gateway to some of the best skiing in the Bearn region, with pistes only 35km from one of the most picturesque

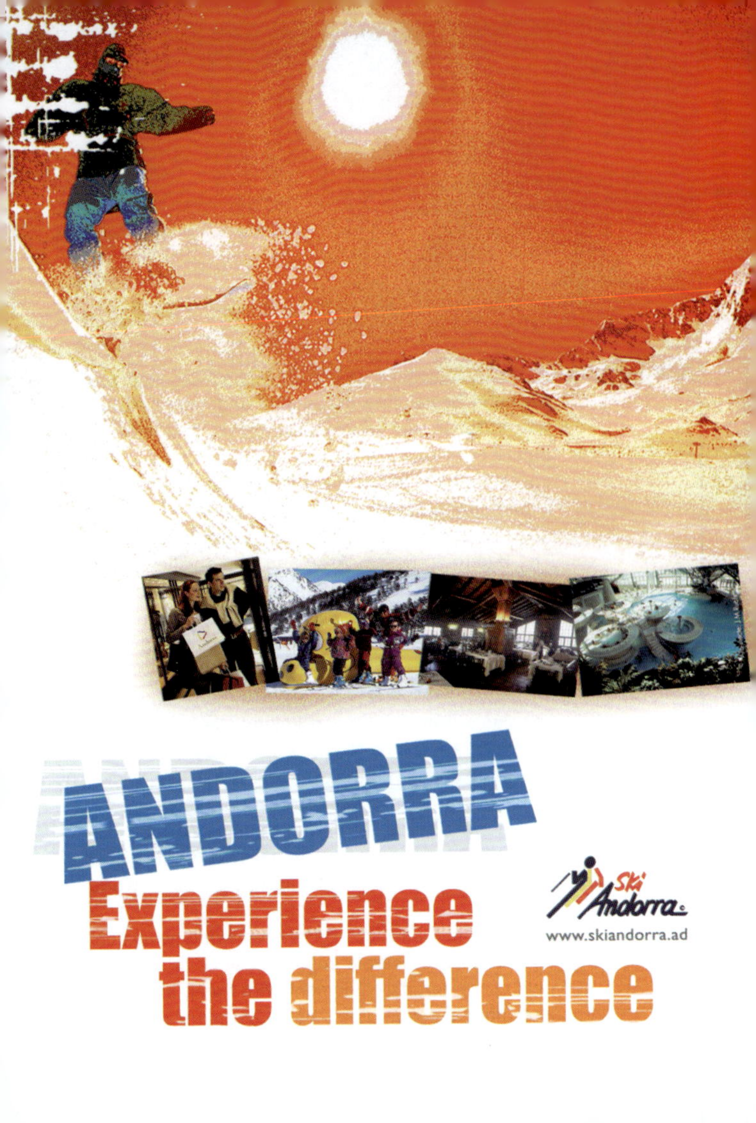
ANDORRA
Experience
the difference
Ski Andorra
www.skiandorra.ad

towns in Bearn, fine restaurants and cosy hotels, it is one of those rare winter-sports bases that also offers plenty of attractions for non-skiing partners and a more authentic local atmosphere than many purpose-built winter-sports resorts

The **Baretous, Ossau, Aspe** and **Soule valleys**, and their five ski resorts, offering fine downhill and cross-country skiing and the Pyrénées National Park, with its breathtaking landscapes, is perfect for snowshoe rambling and mountain skiing.

For skiers from Britain and Ireland, the western Pyrénées are the most easily accessible winter-sports area in mainland Europe, making it feasible to pop over to France for a long weekend on the pistes as well as for a longer skiing holiday. In addition to their accessibility, the western Pyrénées offer some of the most affordable skiing (and après-ski) in the world.

For beginners and for experienced skiers who don't want the added hassle and expense of bringing their own winter sports equipment with them, skis, boots and other essential items of kit are readily available to hire at all the major resorts.

Some of the region's top winter sports are in the **Vallee du Baretous** – nicknamed the 'Valley of the Musketeers' – in the heart of the Pyrénées-Atlantiques, where the magnificent **La Pierre St Martin**, at 1650-2200 metres, has 18 alpine runs (four green, eight blue, five red and one black) and 21 ski lifts, as well as 6.5km of cross-country ski trails. Ideal for families, La Pierre St Martin has a crèche for babies and toddlers and a mini-club for 6-to 12-year olds during school holidays. With 45 new high-pressure snowmakers, skiable pistes are guaranteed both here and at the Vallee du Baretous' 'ski de fond' station, at Issarbe.

Le Somport-Candachu, at 1600-1700 metres, has nine downhill runs and is excellent for cross-country skiing, with 34 kilometres of marked trails that cross the border into Spain, passing through the forests of the Pyrénées National Park.

In the heart of the Pyrénées National Park, **Cauterets-Lys** is a winter-sports village that offers, not only downhill skiing on the **Cirque du Lys**, but also cross-country ski and snowshoe ('raquette') trails, as well as alpine pistes at the **Pont d'Espagne** domain. Forty years old this year, Cauterets-Lys is more than just a ski-station. This picturesque village also offers plenty of off-piste and après-ski life, with health and fitness centres, a cinema, swimming pool, casino and, for families with toddlers who are too young to take to the slopes, a crèche.

Among the other fine winter-sports areas within easy reach of Pau-Pyrénées airport is **Gourette**. With no fewer than 27 runs (five green, nine blue, twelve red and one black) and 16 ski lifts and tows, this is the biggest winter-sports resort in the western Pyrénées. It also has one of the longest downhill slopes in the region and an array of facilities to suit all levels of expertise.

One of the region's better-kept secrets is **Artouste**, a much smaller resort, set in an awesome vista of panoramic snowfields, more than 2000 metres above sea level and overlooked by the towering Pic du Midi d'Ossau. Artouste has a reputation among thrill-seekers as one of the best winter-sports freestyle spots in the Pyrénées.

Pau is also a gateway airport for the super slopes of **Andorra**, the tiny mini-state between France and Spain that has carved itself a high reputation as an affordable but high-quality ski destination. With almost 3000 hectares of skiable snow and 282 kilometres of pistes in three Alpine resorts and one cross-country resort, Andorra offers a total 27 green slopes, 58 blue slopes, 61 red and no fewer than 28 black pistes, all serviced by one of the 107 state-of-the-art lifts. Top winter-sports areas here include **Arinsal**, which is situated beneath the imposing 2569 metre **Pic Negre**, with fine skiing and a lively nightlife. **Pas de la Casa** is the highest resort in the Pyrénées, while the picturesque **Vall d'Ordino** has superb slopes at **Arcalis** and bustling **Soldeu** has a huge range of slopes for snowboarders as well as skiers.

The **Ski Andorra consortium**, comprising all of the tiny principality's main resorts, has a range of ski-passes and other offers, including a five-day pass that's ideal for a short winter-sports break.

SHOPPING

Visitors to Pau with shopping in mind are in for a pleasant surprise. Most French towns offer better quality shopping than British cities of similar size and Pau is no exception. For those in search of retail therapy, the town's shopping streets offer almost everything you could wish for; from hand-made ceramics, tapestries and works of art to antiques and curios, traditional craft products, the latest fashions and, of course, the delicious food and drink of the entire region and, indeed, all of France.

Individual, specialist shops dominate the old town centre, while most of the larger department stores are in the newer part of Pau, between the old quarter and the university district. Huge supermarkets are exiled to the outskirts of the city, where they are easily accessible not only to those staying in Pau but also to holidaymakers staying in the countryside around the city. If you are renting a gîte or a farmhouse and have rented a car, supermarkets such as **Leclerc**, **Geant** and **Intermarche** can all be found just outside Pau and are the most convenient places for your weekly shop for household goods.

For British shoppers, the price tag on many products, including food, drink and clothing, looks quite a bit less than it would be at home. If you are planning a longer trip, it may even be worthwhile travelling light and buying a smart new wardrobe on arrival. If you are looking forward to hiking on Pyrenean trails, camping or fishing in local rivers you will find excellent kit at attractive prices in local specialist outdoor stores and even in some of the large supermarkets.

Credit cards such as Visa and Mastercard are widely accepted in shops and larger stores, but you may be asked to key in your personal identification number or

MAGASIN

Shopping in Pau

present your passport for identification, especially for larger purchases. Charge cards such as American Express are not widely accepted and most market traders, of course, prefer cash.

As a small regional capital, Pau certainly can't match Paris in the haute couture stakes, but it has its share of stylish fashion stores, with designer brands such as **Kenzo**, **MaxMara**, **Armani** and **Karen Millen** on display along Rue Henri IV and the surrounding streets.

The old town is dotted with antique shops packed with everything under the sun, from furniture fit for a farmhouse kitchen or a grand château to paintings, prints and colonial curios. Antique shops cluster around the Château, along Rue Henri IV and on the small streets leading off it. For real antique bargains – or to get an idea of what the dealers are actually paying –

head for one of the regular auctions such as those held at the **Hotel des Ventes Pau-Pyrénées** at the Espace de Bourbon in Pau-Nord, fifteen minutes from the airport. The Hotel des Ventes also handles property auctions. Alternatively, arrange an appointment with the auctioneers at 3 allees Catherine de Bourbon.

For more modern shopping, head for the **Bosquet district** north of the town centre, where you'll find big international and French stores in an up-to-date shopping precinct created during the 1990s with the near total rebuilding of a run-down quarter of the city.

Quirky souvenirs and gifts can be found at **Motors Mania**, on rue Gassion, which celebrates Pau's long-standing passion for aviation and Grand Prix motor sport with a superb collection of impeccable scale-model classic cars, vintage model motor-cycles and historic aircraft models, motor racing posters and other memorabilia. The well-reputed **Gallerie l'Oeil Fauve**, at 7 rue Bernadotte, exhibits and sells fine art by contemporary French painters and other artists and offers a ten per cent discount to Ryanair ticket holders.

Pau and the surrounding villages also have their share of home-grown artistic talent and on the main street of most small towns you will find at least one artist's studio with a gallery of attractive oil paintings, prints or watercolours – perfect to hang on the wall at home to remind you of your trip.

For something more typically Bearnais, you could take home one of the sturdy umbrellas used by Pyrenean shepherds for centuries as protection against sudden downpours and fierce summer sun. Designed for extreme conditions, the shepherd's umbrella is an ideal companion for country walks or a round of golf. With its strong wooden or cane ribs, it is guaranteed not to collapse in a high wind and won't attract lightning like conventional, metal-ribbed umbrellas. You can buy one, or see them being made by Palois craftsmen, at **Parapluie de Berger** on 1 Rue de Lassat.

Another old-fashioned accessory that still makes a useful souvenir or gift is the 'gourde' or leather water-flask, traditionally carried by hunters, shepherds and mountain-walkers. **Arroka**, at 2 Rue du 14 Juillet, is one of only two companies that still make these attractive goatskin bottles, which are now manufactured with a taste-free plastic lining. The traditional sheep-bells for sale here are hammered from a single sheet of copper and make attractive doorbells.

Pau has been a centre for fine tapestry weaving since the Middle Ages, and you can see colourful, modern tapestries being made for sale at the **Atelier Tapisserie d'Art Janine Sipra**, at 8 Rue Salvador Dali. This is a craft workshop where you can commission a unique work from the weavers and learn the rudiments of weaving.

Handmade clothes and soft furnishings are the specialty of **Isabelle Loiseau**, at 1 Rue du Comte de St-Cricq. Out of the city, almost every town and village has its own portfolio of skilled artisans, artists, craft-workers and gastronomic specialists.

In Navarrenx, tapestries and chairs are made to order at **L'Atelier des Ramparts**, in the shadow of the medieval walls at Porte St Antoine. At Sauveterre de Bearn, pretty and practical pottery for the kitchen and dining room is created at **Poterie Parabis** and in Biron, near Orthez, you'll find decorative hand-made brassware being made as it has been for more than sixty years at **Creations Jean Goardere**.

There are retail opportunities in and around Oloron Sainte-Marie too. Pick up a floppy beret (essential for that truly French look) at the **Beatex beret factory,** Rue Rocgrand, or a beautiful Basque linen tablecloth or bedlinen at **Tissages Lartique,** 2 Avenue Georges Messier.

Charming old-fashioned wooden toys and games are made at the **Atelier de Jouets et Meubles en Bois** in Eaux-Bonnes and unique enamelled stoneware can be found at **Ceramiste Sculpteur** in Bilheres en Ossau. In Laruns, **Regards et Visions** at 6 Ch. Bayle displays skilfully-executed landscapes in oils and ink drawings.

Pau and the surrounding Bearn region are famous for products that tickle the taste buds of the most demanding gourmand. The old covered market at **Les Halles,** in the centre of Pau's Place de la Republique, is jam-packed with stores vending the finest produce of the region.

Boulevard des Pyrénées

Out of town, you can sample and buy the famous sweet white wine of the region all along the **Jurancon Wine Route** at: the **Cave des Producteurs du Jurancon** at 53 Avenue Henri IV in Gan (a co-operative cellar which ages and bottles the wines of 300 member vineyards); at the **Commanderie du Jurancon Maison des Vins** in Lacommande; or at the **Confrerie du Jurancon** in Monein. Wine tastings and admission to all three are free. In Pau and around the region (branches in Oloron Sainte-Marie, Orthez, Lourdes, Laruns and elsewhere), look out for the family-run **La Maison Biraben**, with a superb array of foie gras and other fine south-western specialities.

In Pau, the **Bonbons Verdier** sweet factory at 6 rue des Druides is hard to resist. Watch sweets and chocolates being made and take home some of the award winning Verdier 'raisins dores' (golden raisins). Also tempting for the sweet-toothed is **Feerie Gourmande**, at Uzos on the way to Nay. This unique jam and confectionery workshop also features a museum with more than 1,000 exhibits, works of art made from sugar and chocolate and demonstrations by the factory's sweet makers.

Even if you do not intend to buy anything, a visit to one of the dozens of farmers' markets around Bearn is a must, if only to soak up the sights, sounds and smells of a typical French market, where you can find everything from baby rabbits and live chicks to sheep-milk, cheeses, sausage, pates, wild mushrooms and truffles that are literally worth their weight in gold. There are markets almost every day of the week and it's best to get there first thing in the morning to make the most of your shopping, as most of the stall-holders pack up at midday.

No two markets are quite the same. Each market has its own unique assortment of local specialties as well as more run-of-the-mill essentials and, of course, what is on offer also changes with the seasons. In the centre of Pau, the **Place de la Republique** (daily except Sundays and national holidays) is the venue for one of the region's biggest and most colourful farm produce markets, while on Wednesdays and Saturdays there is an organic produce market on the **Place du Foirail**, which is also the venue for a second-hand goods market on Saturday, Sunday and Monday.

There are also markets in **Arudy**, **Nay**, **Salies de Bearn** and **Orthez** on Tuesdays and Saturdays, at **Navarrenx** on Wednesdays and Sundays, and at **Oloron Sainte-Marie** on Fridays. Most markets are morning affairs, but in July and August there are Thursday night markets in the villages of **Laruns** and **Bedous**. It's also worth looking out for posters advertising local 'vide-grenier' jumble sales where people come to offload an eclectic array of second-hand goods, old clothes, antiques and curios.

There's always plenty of junk on offer; from old French Army kit to wooden chests and leather suitcases, brassware, pottery, enamel jugs and old chamber-pots, kitchen-ware, antique tools and cutlery to cast-off video equipment, old records and compact discs, crumbling books and old-fashioned bed-linen and tablecloths. Sharp-eyed buyers may pick up some real bargains. You can pick up a list of loft clearance sales and more up-market antique fairs from local tourist offices. Likely hunting grounds include: Arudy, Salies de Bearn, Laruns and Orthez.

The region also has a lively calendar of themed open-air markets held throughout the year in and around Pau, with traditional Easter and Christmas markets, night markets, regional produce fairs, pottery and craft markets and cheese fairs at venues such as Garlin, Laruns, Monein, Navarrenx, Oloron Sainte-Marie, Orthez, Salies de Bearn and Sauveterre de Bearn. The tourist office in Pau can supply an up-to-date list of events.

ACCOMMODATION

Whatever you plan to do, wherever you plan to go and whenever you plan to arrive, rest assured that Pau and its hinterland have a portfolio of accommodation options that will meet your needs and your budget.

For a special occasion like a cherished anniversary, a first (or second) honeymoon or a romantic weekend, you'll find glamorous châteaux and mansions with their own gourmet restaurants set in landscaped grounds complete with a myriad of luxury touches such as fluffy bathrobes, fine bed-linen and top-quality bathroom amenities. For budget travellers, there are plenty of affordable rooms in both small hotels and bed and breakfast accommodation, while for families and groups there are self-catering farmhouses, gîtes and villas with pools to be rented by the week or by the fortnight.

Finding and reserving a place to stay couldn't be easier. There is a range of organisations offering on-line booking services through several different of web sites, such as **www.ryanair.com**, or by telephone via toll-free numbers with English-speaking reservations staff.

If you are travelling on the spur of the moment and arrive without a place to stay, tourist offices in Pau and around the region will be able to point you in the right direction, with comprehensive lists of all types of accommodation. In short, Pau and the surrounding Bearn region offer an enormous choice of places to stay at prices to suit all budgets, for families, groups of friends, couples and solo travellers.

All accommodation in France – from simple pensions and chambers d'hotes to luxury hotels – is strictly government-controlled and star-rated. This means that it is inspected annually and value for money at all levels is guaranteed.

Travellers with disabilities will welcome the French tourism ministry's 'Tourisme et Handicap' grading system, which rates hotels according to the facilities they provide for people with mobility, visual, hearing and mental disabilities.

A comprehensive list of all accommodation in and around Pau, together with prices and contact details, is available from the **Comite Departemental du Tourisme Bearn-Pays Basque**, 22 ter, Rue J.J. de Monaix, 64000 Pau. Tel: (00 33) 5 59 30 01 30; www.tourisme64.com

Accommodation prices in France are generally lower than in the UK, though they do vary widely across the board, with cheaper accommodation from as little as €20-25 per night and prices of up to €180 per night for four-star accommodation.

Remember that posted prices usually don't include service or government tax, and most do not include breakfast, which is usually a self-service buffet of coffee or tea, juice, rolls, cheese and cold cuts. If you are on a tight budget, you will probably find the same breakfast costs a good deal less in a nearby café than it does in your hotel.

With plenty of accommodation to choose from, you will usually have no difficulty finding somewhere to stay. However, if you plan to visit Pau for a major annual event, such as the town's famous Grand Prix, you will need to book early as rooms can be at a premium.

As well as offering plenty of choice for short-break visitors, Pau has a more than adequate supply of hotels catering for the business traveller and for the meetings, incentive and conference and exhibition markets. The **Hotel Roncevaux**, for example, is very central and within easy walking distance of the Parc Beaumont conference centre.

Chains such as **Ibis, Novotel, Mercure** and **Best Western** are all represented in town, with member properties that offer full business facilities including high-quality communications and conference spaces for small to medium sized business meetings, as well as off-street or secure garage parking.

Many three-star hotels out of town can also offer excellent facilities for the corporate traveller and for small meetings in relaxing surroundings, while for incentive groups there are plenty of venues which can offer activities ranging from golf and trout fishing to quad-biking and white-water rafting.

Until recently, most accommodation in and around Pau has been in two-star and three-star hotels, with eight three-star properties in town offering a total of around 370 rooms and around 650 rooms in the nineteen one- and two-star hotels. The arrival of two new four-star hotels, however, has brought a whole new dimension to accommodation in Pau. The most exciting development on the local hotel scene is the four-star deluxe **Hotel du Parc Beaumont**, recently opened as part of a new urban landscaped project adjoining the beautiful grounds of Pau's **Parc Beaumont casino and conference centre**. Glass, metal and polished wood give this new property (part of the Scandinavian SAS Radisson Hotels group) an appropriately Nordic aura, with eighty rooms including fifteen suites, fifty-three south-facing loggia rooms with views over the Pyrénées, and twelve standard rooms.

For the ultimate in luxury, book one of the top-floor rotunda suites or even the huge presidential suite, with a vast terrace and a 180-degree Pyrenean panorama. General amenities include: restaurant, piano bar, lounges and a fitness centre.

Hotel Continental

This is not the only new hotel venture to open in Pau. The **Mercure group** already has two three-star hotels in town and has now opened the four-star **Mercure Villa Navarre**. This new hotel, which is tipped to bring a touch of boutique hotel style to Pau for the first time, is a charming nineteenth-century English villa set in two hectares of grounds with fine mountain views. The hotel's spacious public rooms are graced by antique mouldings and woodwork. The thirty bedrooms are bright and spacious and facilities include a gym and indoor and outdoor pools.

Outside of town, however, bar a few château-style properties, most local accommodation is in affordably priced three-star hotels. French three-star hotels typically offer a substantial level of comfort and service, with a bar, restaurant, lounge area and in-room facilities such as TV, mini-bar and direct dial phone.

Increasing numbers of three-star properties are members of reputable international hotel brands such as the Best Western chain, represented in Pau by the charming and friendly **Hotel Continental**, on Rue Marechal Foch. Just a stone's throw from the château and Boulevard des Pyrénées, this dignified period building has comfortable rooms with huge bathrooms, small balconies, and all mod cons, at very reasonable rates and, like all Best Western hotels, it's easy to book. Call toll-free on 0800 90 44 90 or go on-line at www.bestwestern.fr.

Independent three-star hotels in and around Pau include: the comfortable Hotel Roncevaux, in the centre of town at 25 rue Louis Barthou; the 22-roomed **Hotel Montpensier** on rue Montpensier; and the attractive **Domaine de l'Aragon**, out of town at Herrere. In the centre of Pau, the **Hotel Bourbon** offers two-star comfort on Place Clemenceau. **Château d'Idron**, at

4 avenue de Beaumont, offers flexible guesthouse accommodation and self-catering facilities, while the two-star **Hotel du Trinquet**, just off the motorway, has 32 rooms situated in lush surroundings. Convenient for the airport is the two-star **Hotel Relais du Luy de Bearn** at Serres Castet, just five minute's drive from the terminal. For something a little more aristocratic, **Domaine de Grand Croix**, 5km south of Pau city centre, is a fine old château that now offers four B&B bedrooms and five self-catering gîtes.

Further afield, the **Auberge de l'Etable** offers tranquillity and rural ambience at Montory, near Oloron Ste-Marie and 45 minutes drive from Pau. You can also enjoy the peaceful French countryside in the little park that surrounds **La Grange du Moulin** at Lescar. Located in a beautiful region, La Grange du Moulin offers quaint, individually decorated rooms and a warm atmosphere. Also outside Pau, the hotel restaurant **Le Fer à Cheval** at Lons can offer guests proximity to the spectacular Pyrenean peaks as well as an authentic taste of regional cuisine.

For those looking for a hotel in Lourdes, the grandest place to stay is the elegant **Hotel de la Grotte**, with its gourmet restaurant. The modern **Hotel Tara**, on the bank of the Gave is another excellent choice. The **Club Hotelier Bearn Pyrénées**, available on-line at www.club-hotelier-bearn.com, has more than 30 member hotels offering two- to five-star accommodation and offers a one-stop selection and reservation service.

Other easy-to-book hotel chains in France include the Ibis consortium, which has cleanly designed, bright, modern hotels all over the country, including hotels in Pau and Lons, and the Novotel group, a chain which is comprised of three- and four-star hotels.

Spa towns, including Pau and nearby Salies de Bearn, have a number of comfortable hotels offering a wide range of health and beauty treatments which can relieve the symptoms of ailments ranging from rheumatism and arthritis to hay fever and skin allergies. The two-star **Hotel du Golf**, at Salies de Bearn, offers easy access to the town's well-known spa treatment centres and is also close to the region's excellent golfing facilities.

At the lower end of the hotel scale, travellers with minimal resources can expect to pay as little as €20-25 for a room in a basic one or two-star hotel, which is unlikely to have en-suite bathroom and WC, but will have shared facilities. Some two-star properties have an en-suite shower and WC but will not usually offer a bath.

A relatively new development on the hotel scene in France is the introduction of the no-frills, minimum

service hotel brands such as **Formule 1**, **Campanile**, and **Kyriad**, among others. These offer comfortable (but tiny) modern rooms, usually sleeping up to three people in a double bed and an upper single bunk, with a tiny shower cabin and WC, at one-star prices. These offer little more than a clean and simple place to lay your weary head. Arriving late at night, with or without a reservation, all you have to do is swipe your credit card in an ATM-style reader outside the front door which will then allocate your room and issue a personal identification number which acts as your key. Almost everything else is automated too, with snack and drink vending machines in the lobby.

Most of these hotels do, however, have a simple breakfast café serving coffee and croissants in the morning. These aren't hotels you'd want to spend a fortnight in, but they are fine for a short break or for the first and last night of a longer tour.

For families or groups of friends planning a longer summer stay in Bearn, the **Gîtes de France** organisation, represented in the UK by the ferry line and holiday company **Brittany Ferries**, or on-line at www.gites-de-france.fr, offers an enormous choice of farmhouse-style holiday homes; more than 1,000 in the Bearn and the neighbouring Pays Basque. Some are small and cosy, others are capable of sleeping up to a dozen. All have at least a small private garden and many have swimming pools and a range of other facilities, usually including satellite TV. Some even have a pool table. These are self-catering properties where you will be expected to do your own cooking and cleaning – and may even have to bring your own bed linen – but staying in a gîte certainly doesn't mean roughing it.

All properties have modern kitchens and most have utility rooms with dishwashers and washing machines. The Gîtes de France organisation also offers a booking service for **chambres d'hotes** (the French equivalent of bed and breakfast), which is ideal for anyone planning a touring holiday. Gîtes de France has members at almost sixty village and countryside locations around the region. Its regional office can be found in the centre of Pau at 20 Rue Gassion: Tel 00 33 5 591120 64.

Also offering self-catering accommodation in chalets, villas, flats and guesthouses is the **Clevacances** organisation, based in Bayonne (4 Allee des Platanes, 64108 Bayonne Cedex: Tel 00 33 5 59 46 52 46: www.clevacances.com).

Place Royale

Another useful name to know is **Logis de France** (www.logis-de-france.fr), a consortium of hundreds of friendly small hotels, which has dozens of members around Bearn. Part of the same organisation, **Logis Rando** is a network of comfortable inns for walkers, located on marked walking trails in and around the Pyrénées. They offer walking advice, a substantial breakfast to set you up for the day, picnic lunches to eat en route and a baggage transport service to take your luggage on to your next overnight stop.

If you fancy a stay on a working farm, contact **L'Acceuil Paysan** (Association Departementale Bearn Pays-Basque: Tel 00 33 59 38 87 29) or **Bienvenue à la Ferme** (Maison d'Agriculture, 124 Boulevard Tourasse, 64078 Pau Cedex: Tel 00 33 5 59 807013: www.alaferme64.com). These two organisations arrange family holidays with Bearnais farmers.

At the top end of the market are upper-crust organisations such as the **Relais & Châteaux** consortium, which represents some of France's most luxurious hotels and restaurants, including the delightful **Domaine de Bassibe** at Segos, 35km north of Pau, with eighteen rooms and suites and a fine gourmet restaurant, and Michel Guerard's **Les Pres d'Eugenie** at Eugenie les Bains, 45km west of town on the borders of Aquitaine, with forty rooms and suites set among aromatic herb gardens.

Châteaux & Hotels de France is another top-notch group. Presided over by leading restaurateur and hotelier Alain Ducasse, this group of charming hotels and restaurants in stately homes includes several properties around Pau: the **Château de Meracq**, a pretty eighteenth-century mansion with eight rooms and suites 21km from town, the modern and stylish **Alysson Hotel** at

Oloron Sainte-Marie, with thirty-two rooms, a big open-air pool and a range of outdoor activities, and the **Pain Adour** and **Herve Garrapit**, both near Mont-de-Marsan, 65km north of Pau.

The stylish **Château d'Izaute** guest house at Caupenne d'Armagnac is pleasant place to stay in the Gers region, with themed suites in lovingly restored nineteenth-century buildings set in spacious, wooded grounds.

Nor should summer visitors dismiss the region's potential for staying under canvas. There are municipal and privately owned and operated campsites throughout Bearn that can offer fabulous locations and great scenery, often on rivers or in lakeside locations. The comfortable facilities include: on-site restaurants, laundries and leisure activities. Many of them even offer luxuries such as open-air swimming pools or are situated next to lakes and rivers for swimming, canoeing and other water sports.
For those who don't want to be weighed down by their own camping equipment, many campsites offer permanent mobile home, cabin or ready-erected tent accommodation. Like hotels, campsites are star-rated.

Around the region, you'll find the two-star **Camping Municipal La Plaine des Sports** in Pau at Boulevard du Cami Salie, the three-star **Camping Beau Rivage** in Navarrenx at Allee des Marroniers, the three-star **Camping de la Source** in Orthez at Boulevard Charles de Gaulle, as well as several other sites at Oloron Sainte-Marie, Morlaas, Salies de Bearn, and Sauveterre de Bearn.

There is a particularly big choice of camping spots in and around Laruns, where you can choose from half-a-dozen two-and three-star sites.

fine french cuisine in a typical, country auberge with a celtic welcome.

Le Kildara Auberge

Hotel – Restaurant

situated on the route of the famous Jurançon wine vineyards in the village of Artiguelouve.

10 min. from Pau Airport.
15 min. from the centre of Pau.
2 min. from Artiguelouve golf course.
5 min. from Gallo-Roman village of Lescar.

Route d'Aubertin, Artiguelouve 64230
Tel. 0559830012 www.lekildara.com

ALYSSON HOTEL

★★★

A charming hotel located in the city and steeped in history. Great comfort, swimming pool, garden, air-conditioned rooms.

Gaelle and Christophe Dodard run the restaurant, serving local cuisine, with a spectacular view of the Pyrénées.

A complete escape to the countryside, only 30kms from airport.

Alysson Hotel, Boulevard des Pyrénées, 64400 Oloron-Sainte-Marie
Tel: 05.59.39.70.70 Fax: 05.59.39.24.47 Email: alysson.hotel@wanadoo.fr
www.alysson-hotel.fr/

HOTELS

BEST WESTERN HÔTEL CONTINENTAL
2, rue Maréchal-Foch
64000 PAU
Tel: +33 (0)5 59 27 69 31
Fax: +33(0)5 59 27 99 84
Email: hotel.continental@libertysurf.fr
Web: www.hotel-continental-pau.com

For business trips or simply for a few days away from it all, choose the Best Western Continental Hotel located in the heart of Pau, the capital of Béarn. Situated in the historic centre of this royal city, at just a stone's throw from the Palais Beaumont, the Casino and the Château of King Henry IV.

HOTEL PARC BEAUMONT
1, avenue Edouard VII, 64000 PAU
Tel: 33-559.118.400
Fax: 33-559.118.500
Email: info@hotel-parc-beaumont.com
Web: www.hotel-parc-beaumont.com
4**** Star Hotel

Exceptionally located in the centre of town, alongside a park. The majority of the rooms have a private furnished terrace with view of the park and the Pyrénées mountains. Gourmet restaurant, bar, relaxation area with heated swimming pool, jacuzzi, sauna, Turkish baths.

HOTEL MONTPENSIER
36, rue Montpensier
Pau, 64000
Tel: +33-559274272
Fax: +33-559274272
Email: Hotel.montpensier.pau@wanadoo.fr

Based in the heart of Henry IV's Royal City in a 19th-century mansion entirely renovated in 2004 and surrounded by a magnificent green belt. The 22 bedrooms have all been individually decorated and have their own unique charms and offer total tranquillity and a touch of elegence.

HÔTEL LE TRINQUET
66 avenue Didier Daurat
64 000 Pau
Tel: 00 33 5 59 62 71 32
Fax: 00 33 5 59 62 09 33
Email: Hotel.letrinquet@wanadoo.fr

A 2-star hotel with 32 spacious rooms, TV, shower/bath, toilets. Friendly bar and restaurant serving local produce. The hotel also has a "trinquet" type of Spanish Pala, 2 squash courts and one tennis court. 10 minutes from Pau airport and Pau city centre and 5 minutes from the racecourse.

L'HOSTELLERIE DU FER À CHEVAL
1 avenue des Martyrs du Pont Long
64140 Lons
(10 mins from the centre of Pau)
Tel: 05 59 32 17 40
Fax: 05 59 72 97 53
English spoken

The Hippodrome, a charming 2-star hotel surrounded by a floral garden. Gastronomie restaurant offering refined traditional and local delicacies in a carefully decorated dining-room. Conference rooms, parties and banquets for 60 people.

LA GRANGE DU MOULIN
Chemin du Batan
64230 Lescar
Tel: +33 688 253920
Fax: +33 559 812901
Email: lagrangedumoulin@club-internet.fr
Web: www.lagrangedumoulin.com

Dominique and Jean-René welcome you all year long in the "Grange du Moulin", an old renewed masonry, subsidery of the Mill of Batan of the 14th century, in the middle of 6 hectares of countryside, only 10 minutes from the centre of Pau.

LE KILDARA
Route d'Aubertin
Artiguelouve 64230
Tel: 0559830012
Fax: 0559830696
Email: info@lekildara.com
Web: www.lekildara.com

A typical french auberge situated in a quaint village adjoining Pau. The restaurant serves fine french food from a rich, varied menu in peaceful surroundings with tree-shaded terrace and garden. The Hotel rooms are quiet and cosy and look onto the neighbouring Jurançon vineyards.

EATING OUT

The right to enjoy fine dining is taken for granted in Pau and the Pyrénées just as it is everywhere else in France. Like every region of France, the Bearn has its own favourite specialities; the farm produce of the rich lowlands, sheep's milk cheese of the Pyrenean pastures and trout and salmon from the rivers that flow through the region.

In addition to the plentiful small, simple restaurants in Pau, there are a few truly stellar establishments around the region. The two-hour lunch break is still virtually sacrosanct in southern France, especially in the summer months, and Pau is no exception. Consequently, most parts of town are studded with restaurants mainly serving affordable lunchtime meals to local people. For the traveller on a budget, these can be great midday value. Most offer a fixed-price menu of two or three courses, often for as little as €10.

Terrasse Château

Wherever you choose to eat, though, it's worth keeping French dining habits in mind and remembering that you're not the only visitor in town. That means finding your lunch table early (around midday), just before the hordes of tourists and local diners descend on Pau's restaurants and brassieres.

Remember, too, that many of Pau's restaurants close after lunch and do not re-open until early evening. You are unlikely to find anywhere serving a full lunch after 1.30pm, though there are plenty of places where you can grab a sandwich or a slice of pizza.

There's much more to the cuisine of Pau and the Bearn than such everyday fare. The traditional **cuisine à la Bearnaise** is hearty. Refined goose fat is preferred to olive oil or butter in traditional rich Bearnais cuisine, while salted or preserved meat is another staple of local cooking

Autumn hillsides

Sauce Bearnaise – a thick sauce of egg yolks, vinegar, shallots, tarragon and white wine blended with butter – is known all over the world and is served with steak or lamb. **Cepes à la mode bearnaise** is an autumnal favourite of wild boletus mushrooms grilled with garlic, parsley and breadcrumbs. **Daube du Bearn** is a rich stew of beef in red wine, while **palombes à la bearnaise** is an even richer dish of wild pigeon marinated in brandy and white wine, then braised in a purée of liver and artichoke.

And let's not forget the most typically Bearnaise dish of all: **poule au pot d'Henri IV**, a glorified chicken casserole named in honour of King Henri IV, who famously promised his subjects 'a chicken in every pot in France' each Sunday lunchtime. Take one boiled chicken, stuff with chopped fresh pork or sausage meat mixed with herbs and eggs, and poach gently with whatever vegetables are to hand.

Another typical dish (very welcome after an energetic day in the country or on the slopes) is **garbure,** something between a very thick soup and a thin stew of preserved goose (trebuc) or duck, salted pork, ham (camot) or bacon, white beans, cabbage and other vegetables. It's never the same two days running.

A bowl of garbure is usually followed by a plate of country ham, black pudding and other sausages, then an even more substantial main course, all rounded off with a taste of **brebis**, the Bearnais sheep-milk cheese, aniseed-flavoured cakes, or light sweet pastries called **merveilles** which are similar to profiteroles.

In addition to farmed beef, lamb, poultry and ham, visiting gourmets will find trout and salmon caught in clear mountain streams such as the Gave de Pau and Gave d'Oloron, which can deliver record specimens. Salt from the Salies region also plays a part in Bearnaise cuisine, and is used for curing ham and sausage.

To go with all these splendid dishes, there are the wines of the region. Bearnais wines have a centuries-old reputation. Henri IV attributed his prowess in battle (and his equally legendary potency in the beds of his

Madiran wine ageing in the barrel

many mistresses) to the rich amber nectar of **Jurancon**. This tart wine is an ideal well-chilled aperitif, and goes well with dessert. There are two styles of Jurancon: the more modern dry version and the traditional sweet Jurancon, which is made by the 'passerillage' method. Just before they are picked, the ripe grapes are pinched off and left to shrivel and sweeten in the sun, increasing their sugar content, which in turn gives Jurancon its hefty fifteen per cent alcohol content.

Diners in the region must also sample **Madiran**, a full-bodied red wine that goes well with the game and red meat dishes of Bearn. Madiran is a product of the northeast of the region, where tannat and cabernet grapes are grown to make this unique wine. In medieval times, Madiran's robustness made it a favourite with pilgrims on the route to Santiago de Compostella, who needed something to fortify them on the long trek over the Pyrénées to Spain.

If your taste runs to lighter wines, try **Pancherec du Vic Bihl**. Like Madiran, this dry, fruity wine comes from the Bearn-Adour vineyards and is produced from a unique combination of grapes. Equally drinkable, especially chilled to the bone on a hot summer's day, are the rose wines of the Bellocq region.

The southwest of France is not famed for its beers, but beer drinkers will find not only the light, crisp lagers traditionally favoured by French drinkers, such as Kronenbourg, but also a long list of imported beers from Ireland, Germany, and Belgium. A stone's throw from the Château, opposite the Table d'Orientation on the Boulevard des Pyrénées, is a cosmopolitan row of

Foie gras

multi-national drinking establishments that includes two Australian-influenced bars, the **Black Bear** and the **Winfield Café** (named after a popular Aussie cigarette brand) as well as two Irish pubs, the ever-popular **Galway**, one of the city's favourite rendezvous spots, and the **Irish Company**. On the same row of terraces, the **Café Russe** is a reminder of an equally cosmopolitan nineteenth-century era when expatriate Russian aristos mingled in the elegant cafés and salones of Pau with British, French and other bluebloods.

Most city centre restaurants have a set lunch menu and Pau also has a plentiful selection of sandwich shops, cafés and snack restaurants, like the very friendly and youthful **Spacy Café**, at the corner of Rue Henri IV, and **Impasse Honset** or **Aux Portes du Château** with a fine view of castle and its courtyard, which serves snacks and light meals all day. **L'Isle du Jasmin** is a stylish teahouse on Rue du Comtat-Biron, immediately beside the castle, with great views of the Pyrénées from its outdoor deckchairs and a tempting selection of cakes, exotic teas, fresh juices and ice cream, while **Le Goxoki** on Place Gramont serves excellent traditional cuisine.

Close to the castle, you'll find plenty of good-quality places to eat crammed together on and around the Rue du Château and its side streets. Look out for **Etna**, an affordable and popular pizzeria; **Au Grain de Raisin**, a cheerful and stylish wine bar and **Restaurant au Fruit de Fondu**, on Rue Sully. **Chez Olive** (9 Rue du Château), **Henri IV** (18 Rue Henri IV) and **La Goulue** (13 Rue Henri IV) are also good bets, each serving some of the best traditional cooking from around the region. Next to Château de Pau, and opposite the Eglise de St Martin, **La Brochetterie** is housed in an old stone building with

Jambon Smoked Ham

Château Quartier

a fine open fireplace and serves superb seafood brochettes and grilled meat dishes, while **Restaurant Le Champagne**, also in the historic centre at Place Royale, is the oldest restaurant in Pau and is regarded as the top place to eat by many discerning locals.

Carnivores will love **La Potence** (40 rue du 14 Juillet, 64000 Pau) for its generous portions of finely matured meats, each accompanied by delicious sauces inspired by the wild herbs that grow on the hillsides of Provence. **Le Donjon** (16 Rue Henri IV) is a combination bar, pizzeria and internet café where you can enjoy a drink and pick up your e-mail while you wait for your pizza. Nearby, at 8 Rue Adoue, **Spago** is a stylish restaurant serving Italian cooking with a decidedly modern twist.

A little way out of town, but well worth the detour, is **Chez Ruffet** (3 avenue Charles Touzet, 64110 Jurancon); a former Bearnaise farmhouse at the foot of the

Jurancon vineyards, where Stephane Carrade, Marc Cazeils and their youthful team present set menus (changed weekly) and à la carte dining inspired by the fine local produce of the southwest. On the outskirts of town, **Au Bon Coin** is another good choice, offering a friendly welcome and three affordable set menus from €11 to €23 per head.

For a takeaway or a quick lunch when more formal restaurants have closed for the afternoon, fast food is represented by a range of brand names; such as the **Buffalo Grill Steakhouse** (2 Avenue Alfred Nobel) and the **Quick** hamburger chain, which has a city centre outlet and drive-through branches at the university and on the main road to Tarbes. The **Tour de Pise** pizza chain has branches at 26 Champetier de Ribes and 6 Boulevard Tourasse. **Le Beret**, on Square George V (off Boulevard des Pyrénées) is a more up-market steakhouse with a regional menu and a fine view of the Pyrénées from its terrace.

Handy for the railway station and buses to the airport is **Au Fin Gourmet** (24 Avenue Gaston-Lacoste) with very reasonably priced à la carte choices and a range of fixed price menus. The Ithurriague brothers, Patrick, Laurent and Christian, serve a Basque-flavoured menu that includes cod, trout, duck liver and Pyrenean lamb.

Further out of town, **Les Pres d'Eugenie** at Eugenie les Bains, owned and run by renowned chef Michel Guerard, has an acclaimed main restaurant which serves a mélange of his ground-breaking cuisine minceur (which changed the face of French cooking a generation ago) along with more robust dishes. River crayfish, steamed trout and lamb are favourites. There's also a smaller, simpler fixed-price restaurant, **La Ferme aux Grives**. Reservations are recommended for either restaurant.

Local sausages and a glass of wine

Reservations are also virtually essential for **Chez Pierre,** one of the grandest and most venerable restaurants in Pau (it celebrates its 80th anniversary this year). Enjoy an apero in the amiably clubby bar before going on to dine in one of the three salons. The well-known chef, Raymond Casau, has a way with fish and his salmon and sole braised in local wines are not to be missed.

One of the city's well-kept secrets (we suspect the canny Palois don't want word about its superb Bearnais cuisine to get out to hordes of foreigners) is **Lou Capetout,** a modest jewel of a restaurant well off the beaten tourist track, north of the town centre (3 Rue Viard). This family-run tavern isn't open every day, so reservations are advised.

Altogether more grand is the **Brasseries les Terasses de Beaumont,** Parc Beaumont, attached to the Palais de Beaumont conference centre. Decorator Jean-Pierre Bouvee recently re-styled the restaurant in gold, red and burgundy and Stephane Carrade, chef of the nearby Michelin one-star Chez Ruffet, presides over the kitchen and a menu inspired by local produce and traditions. In Salies de Bearn, **Hoggs** is a cheerful place to stop for a drink and a bite to eat.

Many restaurants in Pau, as in the rest of France, close for at least two weeks (and even four weeks), usually in August, so if you plan a special trip to one of the region's gourmet restaurants at this time of year you should check that it is be open. If you are unsure of your French, the front desk staff at your hotel will be happy to book a table for you.

Smokers will be relieved to find that few French restaurants have yet followed the lead of Ireland or Norway in banning smoking altogether. Smoking is increasingly restricted in public places in France, but enforcement of no-smoking rules is patchy.

Eating In

For something a little different for those renting a villa or gîte, **La Cuisine de Gilles** offers the perfect way to entertain family and friends at home; a unique gourmet service with a personal touch. Chef Gilles will discuss the evening's menu with you in advance – usually involving traditional dishes with a modern twist using seasonal local produce – cooks for you in your own kitchen and serves the freshly prepared meal. He'll even clean up afterwards!

EATING OUT/EATING IN

AU BON COIN
125 route de Bordeaux
64140 Lons
Tel: +33 (0) 5 59 32 25 99
Fax: +33 (0) 5 59 32 47 84
Web: www.pauboncoin.com

Situated 5 minutes from the airport, 2 minutes from the race course and less than 10 minutes from Pau city centre. Offering you traditional and family-style regional specialties such as Foie Gras, duck breast a l'orange, lamb from the Pyrénées, a selection of dishes from the a la carte menu.

RESTAURANT BAR BRASSERIE
LE CHAMPAGNE
5, place Royale, 64000 PAU
Tel: +33 (0) 559 277 212
Fax: +33 (0) 559 988 659
Email: restaurant@auchampagne.com
Web: www.auchampagne.com

In the heart of Pau's historical centre, on the Place Royale, Le Champagne, one of Pau's oldest establishments welcomes you with its "a la carte" menu offering local delicacies. Menu starting from €15 to €19.50. On a nice sunny day, you can avail of a shaded terrace under the trees of the Place Royale.

LE GOXOKI RESTAURANT
2 place Gramont,
64000 Pau
Tel: 0559 838637

Situated in the very heart of Pau on the Place Gramont, the restaurant Le GOXOKI will serve you its traditional dishes in a relaxing setting. Veal, Gribiche sauce, Lamb Rack, Pig Trotters, Pot au Feu (beef in broth), Parcels of Scallops with Foie Gras.

LA CUISINE DE GILLES
46, rue Montpensier,
Pau
Tel: 05 59 40 34 40
Mobile: 06 81 57 97 40
or his interpreter Don: 06 80 23 61 18
An authentic "Chef" at your service

A pupil of Alain Ducasse of Monaco, having worked for Michel Guerard at Eugenie les Bains and at The Bell Inn at Aston Clinton (Bucks). He is now the caterer and "Chef à Domicile" for the local epicureans. From finger food and canapés to full meals delivered or cooked at your home.

ENTERTAINMENT

Pau's nightlife scene is surprisingly lively; in part because of its large, youthful student population and partly because the town has a long history of providing entertainment and amusement for its foreign visitors. Visiting today, you are spoilt for choice when it comes to deciding where to go after dark. There's plenty of café society, of course, with a number of bars and restaurants providing live entertainment on a regular basis, such as **La Potence** (40 rue du 14 Juillet - see Eating Out), with its jazz dinner concerts on the second Tuesday of every month.

Pick up a copy of the free monthly listings magazine *Cutzine* (available in the tourist office and most bars) for an up-to-date schedule of what's on in and around Pau and as far afield as Biarritz and the coast.

Bigger club-style venues normally levy a cover charge, which includes admission and usually your first drink. You should be prepared for drinks in such places to cost a good deal more than in an ordinary café-bar.

As Pau is a small and compact town, bar hopping on foot is a pleasure rather than a pain. Pau's main nightlife area is aptly nicknamed **the Triangle** and is defined by **Rue Castelnau, Rue Lespy** and **Rue Emile-Garet. Le Caveau**, 18 Rue Castelnau, manages to be lively without being too raucous and attracts a slightly older crowd. A more youthful clientele fills **Le Garage**, 49 Rue Emile-Garet, and the lively **Bearnais**, 3 Rue Lespy, most evenings and both venues are really for those who like their music and conversation loud.

A larger dance floor can be found at the cavernous **Le Paradis**, 11 Place du Forail, which mostly plays a mainstream mix of pop hits and has a moderate cover charge. Even bigger is **Why Not**, the city's premier nightclub in the **Palais des Pyrénées**, which kicks off at midnight and rocks until 6am on Friday, Monday, and Wednesday nights. Check out whynot@wanadoo.fr for details of DJs and guest artists. **El Barrio Libre**, in the central **Quartier Libre** shopping mall, caters to a wide variety of tastes with a ground floor bar and restaurant, a 'Club Privée' on the first floor and facilities for seminars and corporate events as well as private functions.

In Tarbes, the cheerful but classy **Le Moderne** on Place de Verdun is favoured by sporty young locals and rugby fans alike. The Irish-owned **Kildara** pub and restaurant is another lively spot. Located in Artiguelouvre, near the golf course, The Kildara serves a good pint of Guinness and is just 15 minute's drive from Pau.

The nineteenth-century elegance of the **Palais Beaumont**, with its casino, piano bar and restaurant, still dazzles and the tables are open until the early hours for those who fancy a flutter. Roulette, blackjack, boule and a variety of slot machines are all on offer.

Pau has plenty of high culture too. Its new **Conservatoire,** in a gracious former convent building, fosters and presents classical music, while the huge, state-of-the-art **Zenith** concert hall offers pop, rock, jazz and orchestral ensembles year round, as well as hosting festivals of ballet and modern dance by French and internationally-recognised performers. Zenith is also the home of the acclaimed **Pau-Bearn Symphony Orchestra**.

More avant-garde entertainment – musical and theatrical – can be encountered at **La Scene**, Pau's acclaimed performance space at 70 Rue D'Etigny, which hosts bands from the international and home-grown jazz, drum and bass, metal, electro, blues and hip-hop scene. Check it out on the web at www.lascene.free.fr.

There's a similar musical menu on offer at **L'Ampli**, with live and electro beats favoured. The French pop and rock scene is increasingly multi-cultural, with traditional French, Anglo-American and Caribbean influences being balanced by home-grown roots sounds from the former

Orchestre Pau

Villagers in festival costume

French colonies of North Africa and West Africa and from the streets of towns like Lyon and Marseille. A well-known place in Pau to hear some of the newest of these acts is **Abattoirs**, the former slaughterhouse at 64 Rue des Abattoirs de Pau, which is now a large warehouse-style venue for new bands and DJs.

If you visit Pau in June you'll find the Boulevard des Pyrénées and nearby open-air venues such as the courtyard of the Château and the Place Royale awash with musicians for the **Boulevard en Fête** festival, held each year on Midsummer Night's Eve (21 June). Take your pick from cutting-edge DJs, ethnic music, jazz and rock.

There is no shortage of venues for film enthusiasts in Pau. **Le Melies**, 6 Rue Bargoin, is a good spot to aim for with showings including national releases and re-runs of French and international classics from Monty Python's 'Life of Brian' to Fritz Lang's 'Metropolis'. **Mega CGR Pau** is the city's largest and most modern cinema, with twelve screens and excellent acoustics.

SPORT & RECREATION

Whether you are a player or a spectator, Pau and Bearn have more than enough sports and activities to keep you happy however long your stay – and that goes for visitors of all ages. Whether you have come seeking the thunder of galloping hooves at the **Circuit Nogaro** or the famous **Hippodrome** – home to some of France's most prestigious equine and sporting events – the scream of high-tuned engines, the roar of a rugby crowd or the solitary pleasure of angling a tranquil mountain stream, there is something here for you.

Children's activities

Keeping the kids happy on holiday is often a challenge, but it needn't be here. There are fun indoor and outdoor activities for children of all ages, from toddlers to active teenagers. **Pyrénées Aventures Nouvelles** at Aramits offers a range of increasingly challenging activity circuits for children as young as eight years of age as well as for young adults, including climbing and bungee jumping. **La Foret Suspendue**, at Foret du Gourzy (Eaux Bonnes), offers acrobatic treetop rope walks (fifteen of them approved for children) as well as less energetic strolls in a forest environment. **Accrobranches** at Bosdarros, just 15 minutes from Pau and open April to October, is an adventure park that will have the whole family swinging from the treetops!

A little closer to the ground, in the rolling countryside of the Plaine de Nay, the **Espace Loisirs Les Okiri** at Baudreix is perfect for a family outing in the summer, with a lake, beach with lifeguards and 80-metre waterslide, sailing, kayaking, pedalos, tennis and fishing. There are also open-air community swimming pools, most with lifeguards on duty, at Pau, Oloron Sainte-Marie, Navarrenx, Orthez, Monein, Salies de Bearn and a score of other towns and villages around the region.

Pau Golf Club

Golf

Pau is home to France's, and mainland Europe's, oldest golf course. Built for British expatriates in the mid-nineteenth century, the **Pau Golf Club** (at Billere, just outside the city) welcomes foreign visitors. Eight kilometres northwest of Pau on the way to Bayonne, **Golf de Pau Artiguelouve** is a highly rated, 6633-yard eighteen-hole course with excellent facilities. Elsewhere, there is a nine-hole course at **Castepugnon**, in the northern Vic-Bilh region, a twelve-hole course and covered practice range at the **Golf Club de Salies de Bearn** and a four-hectare practice range at the **Golf Club des Vallees** at Oloron Sainte-Marie.

Horse Riding

The region around Pau is proud of its equestrian traditions, from the centuries-old breed of mountain pony traditionally used by shepherds and farmers (and still

used by hill trekkers) to France's first thoroughbred stud, founded at Pau by Napoleon I. There are more than two dozen equestrian centres around the Bearn, including the **Centre Equestre d'Orthez** at Orthez, the **Club Hippique de Lescar** at Lescar and **La Cavaliere** at Salies de Bearn. All of them offer riding lessons for beginners and sessions for experienced riders. There are also numerous farms and trekking centres offering pony and donkey riding and trekking.

Walking

With the Pyrénées not far away, the region offers fantastic potential for walking holidays, with a range of gentler and more challenging walks in the countryside, the foothills or the lovely high Pyrénées.

Mountain sports are hugely popular in the region, with around forty experienced guiding agencies waiting to lead you into the hills. Based in Pau, **Bernard Jamorski** leads summer and winter hikes for all levels of fitness, including snowshoe hiking in winter. From Larudy, **Annie Beaudeant** also leads winter hikes and in summer offers a series of themed wildlife walks in the Pyrénéan National Park.

LE PETIT TRAIN D'ARTOUSTE

THE HIGHEST TRAIN IN EUROPE

Let us take you up...

An easy, magical trip through magnificent mountain landscapes.

★ A PRETTY CABLE CAR, leaving from Fabrèges lake (1200 m), takes you up to la Sagette station, the train's point of departure. A magnificent view of the Pic du Midi d'Ossau and other mountains and over the valley.

★ A RAILWAY JOURNEY along the mountainside through extraordinary landscapes: a 50-minute journey to the Artouste dam.

★ an easy and optional SHORT WALK (10-15 minutes) to the magnificent the Artouste lake.

★ an hour to relax on the BANKS OF THE ARTOUSTE LAKE.

★ the journey back again.

OPEN EVERY DAY from end of May to end of Sept.

→ Informations: 05 59 05 36 99

→ Reservations: 05 59 05 49 61

→ www.trainartouste.com

In Laruns, **Randonnee à la Rencontre des Bergers** introduces you to the vanishing way of life of mountain shepherds in the company of shepherds Made and Stephane. For families with children, **Destination Bearn des Gaves** offers two-night family hikes from farm to farm with a sturdy Basque mountain pony (known as a pottok), and several companies offer donkey trekking holidays. Other guided or way-marked walks include hiking in the Pyrénées National Park (with hotel accommodation in Laruns) or escorted mountain hiking with accommodation in a twelfth-century townhouse in medieval Sauveterre de Bearn.

Grand Prix de Pau

It is possible to walk along the pilgrimage paths across the valleys of the Bearn, or even across the Pyrenean passes (with a car to carry your luggage ahead), or ramble through the wide open spaces of the Aspe Valley in the heart of the Pyrénées National Park. For a full range of walking specialist companies offering accompanied tours contact: Comite Departemental du Tourisme Bearn, 22 ter, Rue J.J. de Monaix, 64000 Pau. Tel: 05 59 30 1 30; www.tourisme64.com

Motor sports

Pau is home to the **Formula 3 Grand Prix de Pau**, the only Grand Prix event other than the Monaco Grand Prix to be run through city streets. Held every year in Pau, this Grand Prix is followed a week later by a unique spectator event, the **Pau Vintage Grand Prix**.

For a more hands-on experience, petrol heads can try out GT Turbo cars or take a one- or two-day circuit-driving course at the **Circuit Pau Arnos**. Elsewhere, there are quad bikes and trail bikes for hire at **Loc'Aventure** in Sainte Colome, where you can learn to handle a quad on 18km of private track or set out on a street-legal quad for a mountain safari around the Bearn. **Planet'Air**, near Navarrenx, has quads and go-karts for children aged six to ten, as well as a quad-bike track for adults and **Sport Evasion Quads 64** at Oloron Sainte-Marie offers introductory quad driving courses for adults and children as well as escorted mountain trips.

Atlantic surf near Biarritz

Watersports

With fast-flowing mountain rivers even in high summer, this is natural white-water rafting and kayaking territory. The **Centre Nautique de Soeix** offers a range of white water activities, including rafting, kayaking, hydro-speed and canyoning with gîte accommodation and introductory packages for beginners. **Destination Bearn** also offers exciting white-water packages on the Gave d'Oloron with guesthouse accommodation.

Surfing is another option. Yes, Pau is miles from the sea, but not that many miles! **Biarritz** (another Ryanair destination) is little more than an hour away by road or rail and has some of Europe's best surfing and sail boarding, with plenty of shops renting equipment. So, if you fancy a day at the beach, it's perfectly possible.

Other activity centres in the region include the exciting **Atmos Phair 64**, with a choice of adrenalin-inducing sports and activities, and **Escary Decouverte**, at Aramits, where you can learn to fly micro-lights and light aircraft, go quad-riding and karting, and make a tandem parachute descent from 3000 metres.

Angling

Mountain rivers fed by snow-melt meet slower-flowing watercourses near Pau, and the region is well known for its record-breaking trout and salmon. Experienced guides can lead you to the best fly-fishing trout waters of the **Aspe Valley** (reservations through Aspe Tourisme: Tel 05 59 34 57 57) or the **Bearn des Gaves**. The Gave d'Oloron is prize salmon territory, with weekend and one-week fishing packages available (Destination Bearn des Gaves: Tel 05 59 65 03 06).

Also in the Bearn de Gaves are black bass lakes, while there is night fishing for carp in the waters of the Gave de Pau and a variety of manmade lakes. For a free fishing map of the entire region, contact the Comite Departemental du Tourisme Bearn, 22 ter, Rue J.J. de Monaix, 64000 Pau. Tel: 05 59 30 1 30; or visit their website www.tourisme64.com

Cycling

Bearn has a huge choice of routes and itineraries for mountain-bike fans, and mountain bikes can be hired round the region. In Pau, you can rent bikes at **Romano Sport** (1 Rue Jean Revell) or **Cyclo 2000** (1 Rue Paul-Jean Toulet). **Bernard Jamorski** (12 Rue Samonzet) offers group mountain-biking trips in the Pyrenean foothills and on even more challenging mountain routes.

Rugby

Rugby supplants soccer as the favoured spectator sport of southwest France and virtually every town and village fosters its own local team. More than a few French international players hail from these parts. For a list of local fixtures and venues, ask the local tourist office or check out local newspapers.

Quilles and boules

In much of France, it's the age-old sport of **boules** (or petanque) that is played on most village squares in

Rugby, popular in the South

Elan Bearnais Pau-Orthez

summer and visitors are welcome to join in village tournaments, though you're unlikely to beat the locals. In Pau, there's a game with an even more venerable pedigree.

Quilles (ninepins) is played indoors in a hall known as a plantier. It's an ancestor of modern-day bowling played with massive skittles standing almost a metre tall and weighing three kilograms and an equally hefty ball carved from walnut and weighing almost six kilograms. You'll find quilles halls in Pau and Monein and at other villages around the Bearn including Mazerolles and Malaussanne.

Basketball

Basketball is a local passion, and Pau is home to one of France's top two clubs, **Elan Bearnais Pau-Orthez** (winners of seven French championship titles and one European Cup). The home stadium attracts fanatical crowds of local supporters.

SPORTS & RECREATION

HARAS NATIONAL DE PAU-GELOS
Service Visites "Les Amis du Haras"
64110 Gelos
Tel: +33(0)5 59 35 06 52
Fax: +33(0)5 59 35 06 52
Email: amisduharas@aol.com
Web: http://ahnpg.free.fr/

Welcome to this 18th-century mansion house with a park of 30 acres. Its stables house English and Arab pure breeds, draughhorses, local ponies and the famous anglo-arab crossbreed which originated in the Pau area. Collection of coaches of the 19th century.

ACCROBRANCHES
in BOSDARROS 15mn from Pau
Would You Like To Experience Strong Sensations?
You will be able to tread on the Giant's Swing, climb the Vertical Net, do Tarzan's Jump, cross the Himalayan Bridge and finish off with the Tyrolian Suspended Slide. It will take your breath away.... For all ages.
« Vert Voltige Cordes »
Bookings Tel : 05-59-21-68-11
Open from April to October
E-mail: EpiComGaveCoteaux@cdg-64.fr
Web Site : www.cc-gavecoteaux.fr

ESCARY
A conference like no other...
4 fully equiped conference rooms with air conditionning
Sporting facilities in house
(2000 Ha):
Quad, 4X4, Cross country
Karting, Mountain bike,
Horse riding, Clay Pigeon
shooting, helicopter, ULM
Françoise & Philippe
DUBERN
Domaine ESCARY
64 570 ARAMITS
Tel: 0033 (0)5 59 34 11 34
http://www.escary.com
Email:contact@escary.com
ESCARY

ENGLISH	FRENCH	GERMAN	SPANISH	ITALIAN
GREETING & PHRASES				
hello	bonjour	hallo	hola	ciao
how are you?	comment allez vous?	Wie geht es Ihnen	¿como estás	come stai?
goodbye	au revoir	auf wiedersehen	adiós	arrivederci
I like	j'aime	ich möchte	me gusta	mi piace
thank you	merci	danke	gracias	grazie
please	s'il vous plaît	bitte	per favor	per favore
DIRECTIONS				
behind	derrière	hinten	detrás	dietro
beside	à côté de	neben	al lado	accanto
help	l'aide	die Hilfe	ayuda	aiuto
in front	devant	vor	en frente	davanti a
left	à gauche	links	izquierda	a sinistra
lost?	perdu	verloren	perdido	perduto
right	à droite	rechts	derecha	destra
straight ahead	tout droit	immer geradeaus	todo recto	diritto
telephone	le téléphone	das Telefon	teléfono	telefono
ticket	le billet	die Karte	billete	biglietto
tourist office	le syndicat d'initiative	die Touristeninformation	información turística	ufficio turistico
turn	tournez	abbiegen (as in 'to turn left')	girar	girare
SITES				
castle	le château	das Schloss	castillo	castello
cathedral	la cathédrale	der Dom	catedral	cattedrale
church	l'église	die Kirche	iglesia	chiesa
library	la bibliothèque	die Bibliothek	biblioteca	biblioteca
museum	le musée	das Museum	museo	museo
statue	la statue	die Statue	estatua	statue
tour	la visite	die Tour	visita	gita
tower	la tour	der Turm	torre	torre
SHOPS AND SERVICES				
bank	la banque	die Bank	banco	banca
newsagents	le tabac-journaux	der Kiosk / das Zeitschriftengeschäft	quisco	Tabacaio/Giornalaio
pharmacy	la pharmacie	die Apotheke	farmacia	farmacia
pub	le pub	die Kneipe	pub	pub
restaurant	le restaurant	das Restaurant	restaurante	ristorante
shopping centre		das Einkaufszentrum	centro comercial	centro commerciale
supermarket	le supermarché	der Supermarkt	supermercado	supermercato
EMERGENCY				
accident	l'accident	der Unfall	accidente	incidente
assault		der Überfall	asalto	assalto
doctor	le docteur	der Arzt	médico	dottore
hospital	l'hôpital	das Krankenhaus	hospital	ospedale
injury	la blessure	die Verletzung	herida	ferita
police	la police	die Polizei	policia	polizia
thief	le voleur	der Dieb	ladrón	ladro

ENGLISH	FRENCH	GERMAN	SPANISH	ITALIAN
EATING OUT				
beer	la bière	das Bier	cerveza	birra
bill	l'addition	die Rechnung	la cuenta	conto
bread	le pain	das Brot	pan	pane
butter	le beurre	die Butter	mantequilla	burro
chicken	le poulet	das Huhn / Hühnchen	pollo	pollo
coffee	le café	der Kaffee	café	caffé
dessert	le dessert	der Nachtisch	postre	dolce
fish	le poisson	der Fisch	pescado	pesce
food	la nouriture	das Essen	comida	cibo
fruit	le fruit	das Obst	fruta	frutta
meat	la viande	das Fleisch	carne	carne
menu	le menu	das Menü	menu	menu
milk	le lait	die Milch	leche	latte
sandwich	le sandwich	das Sandwich / das belegte Brötchen	bocadillo	pannino
snack	le snack	der Imbiss	aperitivo	sputino
soup	la soupe	die Suppe	sopa	minestra
tea	le thé	der Tee	té	té
tip	le pourboire	das Trinkgeld	propina	mancia
vegetables	les légumes	das Gemüse	verdura	verdure
water	l'eau	das Wasser	agua	acqua
NUMBERS/ TIME				
hour	l'heure	die Stunde	hora	ora
minute	la minute	die Minute	minuto	minuto
second	la seconde	die Sekunde	segundo	secondo
this afternoon	cet après midi	heute Nachmittag	esta tarde	questo pomeriggio
this morning	ce matin	heute Morgen	esta mañana	questa mattina
today	aujourd'hui	heute	hoy	oggi
tomorrow	demain	Morgen	mañana	domani
yesterday	hier	gestern	ayer	ieri
one	un(e)	Eins	uno	uno
two	deux	Zwei	dos	due
three	trois	Drei	tres	tre
four	quatre	Vier	cuatro	quattro
five	cinq	Fünf	cinco	cinque
six	six	Sechs	seis	sei
seven	sept	Sieben	siete	sette
eight	huit	Acht	ocho	otto
nine	neuf	Neun	nueve	nove
ten	dix	Zehn	diez	dieci
DAYS OF THE WEEK				
Monday	lundi	Montag	lunes	lunedi
Tuesday	mardi	Dienstag	martes	martedí
Wednesday	mercredi	Mittwoch	miércoles	mercoledí
Thursday	jeudi	Donnerstag	jeuves	giovedí
Friday	vendredi	Freitag	viernes	venerdi
Saturday	samedi	Samstag	sábado	sabato
Sunday	dimanche	Sonntag	domingo	domenica

INDEX – QUICK FIND

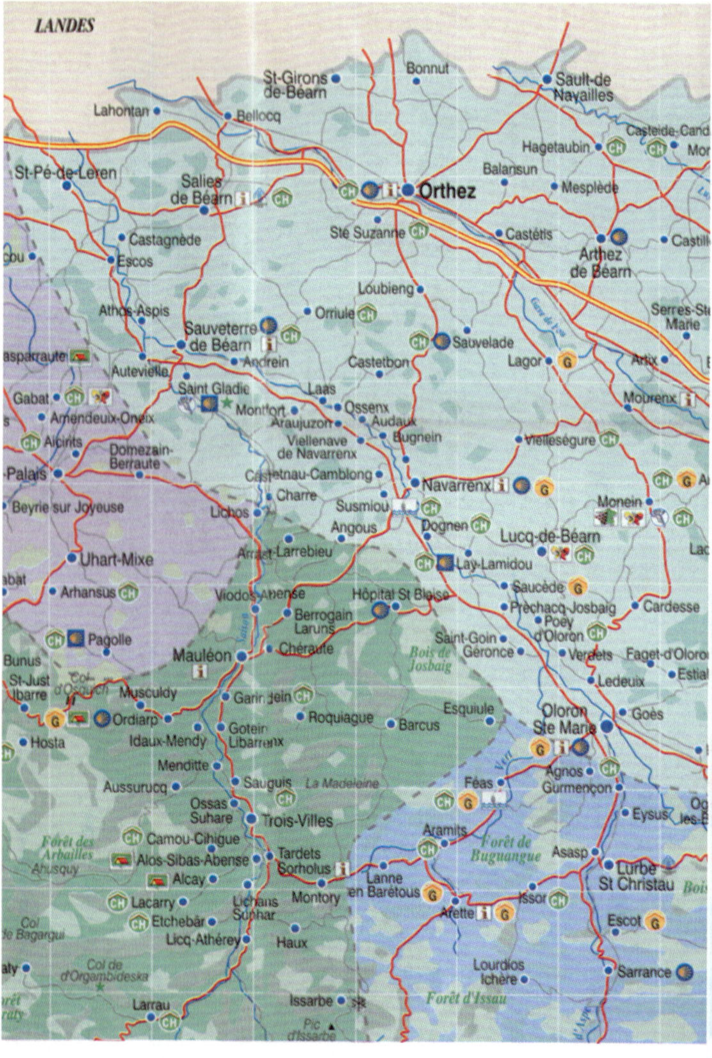

LANDES
St-Girons de-Béarn
Bonnut
Sault-de Navailles
Lahontan
Bellocq
Hagetaubin
Balansun
St-Pé-de-Leren
Salies de Béarn
Orthez
Mesplède
Castagnède
Ste Suzanne
Castétis
Escos
Arthez de Béarn
Loubieng
Athos-Aspis
Orriule
Serres-Ste Marie
Sauveterre de Béarn
Sauvelade
Andrein
Castetbon
Lagor
Artix
Autevielle
Saint Gladie
Laas
Mourenx
Gabat
Montfort
Ossenx
Amendeux-Oneix
Araujuzon
Audaux
Aïcirits
Viellenave de Navarrenx
Bugnein
Viellesègure
Domezain-Berraute
Castetnau-Camblong
Navarrenx
Charre
Monein
Beyrie sur Joyeuse
Lichos
Susmiou
Angous
Dognen
Lucq-de-Béarn
Uhart-Mixe
Arrast-Larrebieu
Lay-Lamidou
Arhansus
Viodos-Abense
Hôpital St Blaise
Saucède
Berrogain Laruns
Préchacq-Josbaig
Cardesse
Poey d'Oloron
Pagolle
Saint-Goin
Mauléon
Chéraute
Bois de Josbaig
Géronce
Verdets
Bunus
Ledeuix
St-Just Ibarre
Col d'Osquich
Musculdy
Garindein
Esquiule
Oloron Ste Marie
Goès
Ordiarp
Roquiague
Barcus
Hosta
Idaux-Mendy
Gotein Libarrenx
Menditte
Agnos
Vert
Féas
Aussurucq
Sauguis
La Madeleine
Gurmençon
Ossas Suhare
Trois-Villes
Eysus
Aramits
Forêt des Arbailles
Camou-Cihigue
Forêt de Buguangue
Asasp
Ahusquy
Alos-Sibas-Abense
Tardets Sorholus
Lurbe St Christau
Alcay
Lanne en Barétous
Lacarry
Lichans Sunhar
Montory
Issor
Arette
Etchebar
Escot
Col de Bagargui
Licq-Athérey
Haux
Col de d'Organbideska
Lourdios Ichère
Sarrance
Larrau
Issarbe
Forêt d'Issau
Pic d'Issarbe

GERS
Malaussanne
Portet
Garlin
Castetpugon
Aydie
Mont-Disse
Piets
Maison du Jambon de Bayonne
Arzacq Arraziguet
Mascaraàs-Haron
Arrosès
Tadousse
Cadillon
Meracq
Garos
Vialer
Séméacq-Blachon
Garlède
Lannecaube
Arricau Bordes
Moncaup
Lonçon
Carrère
Thèze
Coslédaa
Escurès
Momas
Sévignacq
Lembeye
Casteide Cami
Caubios Loos
Lasclaveries
Juillacq
Navailles Angos
Bougarber
Sauvagnon
St-Armou
Momy
Castéra Loubix
Serres Castet
Maure
Casteide-D
Aussevielle
Pontiacq-Viellepinte
Lescar
Morlaàs
Sedze Maubecq
Andoins
Espéchède
Laroin
Arrien
Eslourenties
PAU
Jurançon
Gelos
Idron
Aast
Artiguelouta
Aubertin
Saint-Faust
Nousty
Assat
Gomer
Ger
Espoey
Angaïs
Bordes
Gan
Hours
Livron
Lasseube
Boeil Bezing
Beuste
Bosdarros
Lagos
Nay Bourdettes
Baudreix
Pontacq
Haut de Bosdarros
Lasseubetat
Coarraze
Rébénacq
Igon
HAUTES PYRÉNÉES
Buziet
Asson
St-Vincent
Buzy
Lys
Bruges
Lestelle Bétharram
Gave d'Ossau
Sévignacq-Meyracq
Grottes de Bétharram
LOURDES
Ste-Colome
Arudy
Iseste
Louvie Juzon
Arthez d'Asson
Plateau du Bénou
Castet
Bilhères d'Ossau
Bielle
Gère-Bélesten
Aste-Béon
TOULOU

VERS BORDEAUX
Université
VERS BAYONNE
VERS OLORON
Rue Beverly
R. Chantilly
Avenue Fouchet
Léon Bérard
Av. du Doyen
Allées Condorcet
R. Saint Exupéry
Av. de la Maisonce
Rue Laborde
Rue de Montardon
R. du Balaïtous
Mohedan
Av. de L'Université
Avenue Jean Mermoz
Av. Trianon
Rue de Rouen
Rue des Rosiers
Boulevard Recteur Jean Sarrailh
Avenue Dufau
Cours Lyautey
Av. Kennedy
Montilleul
Avenue d'Este
R. des Tamaris
Château
Avenue Beziou
Rue Cazalis
Av. Mirabelle
Rue Léonard Constant
Av. de l'Eglise Saint Joseph
Rue du Baron Séguier
R. Lamaignère
Av. des Frères Wright
Bd Alsace Lorraine
Rue de l'Abbé Brémond
Bd Edouard Herriot
Parc des Expositions
Bd Champetier de Ribes
Avenue de la Résistance
Rue Viard
R. Capit. Guynemer
R. de Bordeu
Rue des Dames St Maur
Boulevard Alsace
Rue Bourbaki
Place du Foirail
Rue de Boyrie
Rue Gaston Phoebus
Rue Victor Hugo
Rue A. Ducasse
R. J. D'arc
Allée Lamartine
Rue Michelet
Av. Ed. Rostand
Rue Carrère
Rue Pasteur
Rue Carnot
Rue Montpensier
Rue O' Quin
Rue Jean Réveil
Rue Michel
Rue des Anglais
Rue Castetnau
Rue Lespy
Cours Camou
Rue du Maquis de Béarn
Bordelongue
Caserne Bernadotte
Allée du Grand Tour
Rue de Liège
Rue de Monpezat
Rue d'Orléans
Place de la Libération
Pl. de la République
Halles
Rue de la République
Place des 7 Cantons
Rue Emile Guichenné
Centre Bosquet
Cours Bosquet
Rue Serviez
Rue Bayard
Rue d'Etigny
Place Gramont
Rue Marca
Rue Mal Foch
Rue des Cordeliers
Préfecture
Rue Mal Joffre
Place Clemenceau
Place St Louis de Gonzague
Boulevard
Rue Henri IV
Rue Louis Barthou
Place Royale
Boulevard des Pyrénées
Funiculaire
Avenue Jean Biray
Avenue Napoléon Bonaparte
Avenue Gaston Lacoste
Rue du Gave
Rue des Fontaines
Roussille
Rue du 14 Juillet
Rue M. Barthou
Rue Gal Dauture
Gloxin